How To Create Wealth Investing In Real Estate

By Grant Cardone

How To Create Wealth Investing In Real Estate

Contents

Preface

Preface

Grant Cardone has been investing in real estate for over thirty years across the United States. As this book goes to press, his company, Cardone Capital, currently has 5,000 units under ownership and over one billion dollars in real estate holdings.

After earning his accounting degree from McNeese State College, Mr. Cardone found himself in a career that he did not see leading him to true legacy-building wealth. What would later become one of his signature responses to adverse situations, Cardone doubled-down and not only mastered sales but created an entirely new sales approach, strategy, and technique.

At thirty-one years old, Grant Cardone was credited with transforming the sales process of an entire industry.

Since then, he has worked with some of the largest Fortune 500 companies in the world on how to increase revenue and improve their customer experience.

He currently operates seven privately-held companies with affiliates and offices around the globe. His business interests range from real estate, sales and marketing training, coaching and consulting, to social media. His companies have earned numerous business awards and accolades. And, Forbes Magazine named him as "The Number-One Business Influencer to Watch".

Cardone's career in real estate had a less than auspicious start with an investment in a single-family home. Quickly learning that this approach to real estate wouldn't work, he transitioned to multifamily units. As he progressed in real estate investing, his deals became larger and larger. Today, Mr. Cardone has become well-known in the real estate world.

To allow friends and family to invest alongside him, he founded Cardone Capital and recently opened three successful fund offerings, all of which were over-subscribed in record time. He currently has several more funds being offered or in development.

In addition to being a hands-on CEO, Cardone is also a New York Times bestselling author of seven books and his sales training courses have educated over fifty million students. He is a contributing writer to CNBC, Entrepreneur.com, Forbes and Business Insider, as well as a regular guest on Fox News, Fox Business, CNBC, and MSNBC.

With all his success, Mr. Cardone says his proudest accomplishments are his marriage of fifteen years to Elena Cardone, their two children, Sabrina and Scarlett, and the time he invests in giving back to the community through his philanthropic endeavors, which have raised over two hundred million dollars for charities.

Introduction

Introduction

As long as I can remember, I have been fascinated with real estate. I have been drawn to it for my entire life; and for the last 30 years I have been buying apartments. It didn't matter whether it was a piece of land, a house, or a store front, I have always had an affinity for real estate and I also had some basic understanding that real estate was valuable.

I remember my Dad would drive my Mom and us five kids around on the weekends looking at real estate. My Dad owned three homes during his lifetime, and each one represented the fact that he was going somewhere, succeeding with each move. Just a few years before my Dad died he bought his dream house and he told Mom, *"We've made it."* It was almost two acres, on the waterfront, had lots of big trees, and was in a neighborhood filled with doctors and lawyers and people who belonged to the local Country Club.

When he died, my Mom had to immediately sell the dream house because it was too much for her to manage. That was a huge lesson that I would not fully understand until I started investing in real estate myself, many years later, and one you must understand if you are going to create financial freedom using real estate. But, more on that later.

As an aspiring young teenage boy, when I started reading books about wealthy people, I noticed how many of them owned real estate. I remember running across a study done about the real estate holdings amongst the super-rich in America. It suggested households who owned large amounts of real estate had lower educational levels, were not significantly associated with inheritance, were not socially connected, and did not have some special occupational status. That describes me perfectly.

I didn't have a fancy education, my Dad didn't give me a million to start, like *"The Donald"*, I definitely wasn't connected, and I had never held a high-level corporate job title or had some great tech idea I could bring to Silicon Valley.

Throughout history, real estate has proven a viable investment vehicle and has been validated by some of the wealthiest families, even institutions, on the planet. Those that control the real estate end up with wealth. And by the way this is not a new thing. The great civilizations of the Romans, Egyptians, Greek, Chinese, Persians, and Mayans, all had massive real estate holdings as part of their power structure. In the 1920's, the British were reported to own 25% of the world's land mass.

Here is a little hidden fact for you, known only once you get big in the game of real estate investing: The largest insurance companies in the world love commercial real estate and use income producing real estate to ensure they are able to pay off the death and retirement benefits of its premium holders. At Cardone Capital, we will access insurance companies to partner with us in transactions, reducing the cost of debt and improving our returns. The insurance companies use the dependability of the income from the real estate to improve their returns and pay off beneficiaries when necessary.

Research history and you will see lots of super wealthy people using real estate to either create wealth, preserve it, or both. John D. Rockefeller started in oil and ended up controlling massive amounts of real estate, making him the richest man in the world. Some say when you adjust for inflation he would still be the richest man in the world by many times.

John Jacob Astor invested in Manhattan real estate and in today's terms would be worth $138 billion, more than Jeff Bezos, founder of Amazon. A more recent example is Donald Bren in Orange County, California, now considered the richest real estate developer in the United States. He started investing in real estate in his fifties. Or how about Stephen Ross, here in Miami, owner of the Related Companies, who borrowed money from his mother and dipped his feet into affordable housing? He is now worth $12 billion and owner of the Miami Dolphins and Hard Rock Stadium.

Then, there is outspoken Sam Zell, worth $5 billion, who started buying and fixing affordable apartments in secondary markets. He went on to create one of the biggest real estate investment vehicles in the world, allowing others to invest alongside him. Sam has made billions of dollars for himself and others. Sam Zell is who I am modeling Cardone Capital after.

Of course, I must mention Donald Trump, President of the United States. Mr. Trump is worth $4 billion, his name is on luxury buildings and golf courses in New York, Chicago, Miami and around the world. Whether you like *"The Donald"* or not, pay attention to how he got his start. Donald's Dad, Fred Trump, didn't get started in luxury real estate. Fred built 4,000 affordable rentals for servicemen returning from the war, and ended up owning 27,000 units. Multiply 27,000 units times any monthly rent, and you quickly see how anyone can produce tremendous wealth over time while the earth beneath the apartments becomes more valuable (appreciates).

Andrew Carnegie, the wealthiest man in America during the early 20th Century, once said, *"Ninety percent of all millionaires become so through owning real estate."* He went on to say, *"More money has been made in real estate than in all industrial investments combined."*

Ray Kroc, who held a minority position in a company called McDonald's, figured out if he controlled the real estate beneath each of the McDonald's franchise locations, selling french fries and milkshakes, he could get control of the company. It worked and the original founders of McDonald's surrendered the worldwide franchise ownership over to Ray Kroc, who built the largest restaurant chain in the world.

I am going to give you one last example because it blew me away. Arnold Schwarzenegger, Mr. Universe, The Terminator and Governor of California, now worth $300 million, did not make his first money as a weightlifter or as an actor. In 1970, he was using all his surplus money to invest in buying apartments in Santa Monica and soon became a millionaire as an apartment investor. The income from the apartments allowed Arnold to create financial freedom so he could focus on his acting career.

Clearly, you can tell I love real estate. But what attracts me the most is that every time I meet successful real estate investors I notice they have a different lifestyle and freedom than other business people. They seem less stressed, calmer, and overall more relaxed.

Even during the housing collapse of 2007-2009, without question the most severe real estate contraction since the great depression, those invested in real estate didn't sweat it. They didn't like it, but they knew it would pass. And by the way, it did pass. If you owned apartments during the worse part of the greatest housing bust in our history and even if you were buying at the top of the market at that time, your investments would be worth more today than they were when you bought them.

Louis Glickman, a well-known real estate investor, made popular the saying, *"The best investment on Earth is earth."* If I could tweak Mr. Glickman's quote, I would say, *"The best investment on Earth is earth that produces cash flow."*

If you study the people listed above they weren't the smartest students, had minimal political connections early on, no technology background, no patents, no franchises, and were not complex strategists. What they all do seem to have in common is they were all fairly simple in their approach, hard workers, frugal, risk-adverse, and made big bets on real estate that produced real income.

My real estate investing career is limited to buying cash flow producing real estate in good markets. To date, I have bought and sold almost $1 billion of real estate over my career and I currently control about $700 million in properties. Hopefully, by the time you finish reading this book, that number will have gone up.

It all started with one deal; in fact, it all started with one bad deal. My first purchase was a $78,000 single-family home and as I write this, I am under contract on three deals that total almost $300 million putting me over $1 billion in holdings. Mind boggling, right?

My goal in the beginning was to accumulate 20 units and make $100,000 a year in passive income from the properties, and at that time, I knew nothing. Now, the goal is 10,000 units, change the way people invest in real estate, and to one day take my holdings to Wall Street as a REIT.

Why I Wrote This Book

Why I Wrote This Book

My main goal with this book is to 1) convince you to start investing in real estate that pays, 2) show you how to get started buying deals, and 3) prevent you from making costly mistakes. This small book clearly cannot answer every question you might have, but will get you on your way. Remember another quote from Andrew Carnegie, *"The wise young man or wage earner of today invests his money in real estate."*

If you are an experienced investor, you may find some of this elementary, but I assure you that even the most advanced investor will learn some strategies we employ at Cardone Capital that improve our returns to our investors, increase positive cash flow, and assure us of 2X and 3X returns.

"The wise young man or wage earner of today invests his money in real estate."
- Andrew Carnegie

What you will see me do here, is make a case for why income-producing real estate is probably the most secure investment available today for everyday hardworking people and to help you sort out and simplify the kinds of deals you should be buying. I will also show you how to find deals, assess their value, and how to buy the right deal.

If you don't want to go it alone and would like to be involved in larger deals from the get go, you should definitely look into what we are doing at Cardone Capital, where we are changing the way people invest in real estate. I created Cardone Capital not to play the game, but to change the game of real estate investing for large and small investors.

The fact is, the little guy almost never gets the great deals because most investors don't know what to look for, who to call, and where to get the best debt. I want to help you get in the game of real estate investing and the more knowledge you have, the more confidence you will have to invest.

One last thing, and something I will repeat over and over in this book: I believe investing in cash flow positive real estate may prove to be the best financial decision of your lifetime; I know it has been for me.

Of all my businesses, my real estate business provides me with the most financial security. The other six businesses are great, and I value each of them very much, but none of them offer the advantages real estate investing provides. Investing in income- producing real estate provides leverage, cash flow, tax advantages, and explosive upside.

And while real estate needs attention, like any business, I assure you, when you purchase the right size properties, in the right locations, with the right debt, and assign the right management team to handle the properties, this investment will still prove to be less work than an ordinary business. More importantly, 10 to 20 years from now, someone will pay to live in and use the properties we are investing in today.

If I died tomorrow, my real estate holdings will produce income for my wife, kids and the charities I love for decades to come. That's right, long after I am done with this body, my real estate holdings will continue to fund a lifestyle for my wife, kids, their kids, my church, charities, and whatever I direct the estate to do with the free cash flow produced from the properties. This is called generational or legacy wealth.

But you may not be thinking about generational wealth at this point. You may just be getting started, so I want to simplify apartment investing for you and help you avoid the mistakes I see most people make. By avoiding these mistakes, you can make sure your first deals work and you will be off to a great start. To do that you need to know what you are looking for, what works, what to avoid that doesn't, how to find the right deals and then how to buy, manage and sell them.

If you have been dabbling with smaller deals or single-family residences, my goal for you is to open your eyes up to how to invest at levels that can truly change things for you and your family.

I want to help move you from the landlord collecting more headaches than rent, to a knowledgeable investor who knows how to create a real business around real estate. My goal is to change the way you think about and approach real estate investing, so you aren't buying deals that never create financial freedom for you.

I want you to understand how I see a deal and why I invest ALL my money in these types of assets. You should know what I know so you can have the confidence to invest with me. Cardone Capital is for those who love the idea of real estate investing, but don't have time, because they're juggling their primary business and family, to ever get around to finding deals, getting brokers on the phone, and managing tenants.

At Cardone Capital, we are allowing everyday people access to extraordinary deals and changing the entire industry of real estate investing, where the big guys get all the great deals and the little guys get the left overs. And that, by the way, is a fact you already understand, or you will take my word for, or you will learn the hard way.

Keep in mind while reading this that I openly detest Wall Street stocks, 401k's, and bond investing. I despise the banks, who pay almost nothing to hold my cash, and then lend it out at 9X. Also, it is important you understand my mindset: I am a complete coward when it comes to investing and I never speculate; I refuse to lose money.

I only invest my free cash (extra money) in one thing: real estate. And I only invest in real estate that produces income. A very successful business man in London recently asked me, *"How much should I invest with you?"* My answer was, *"Everything!"* How can I tell someone that? Because, I have everything I have created, invested in real estate, because I believe in the fundamentals that make it viable long term.

Remember, I don't speculate and I don't gamble with my hard earned money. I have worked very hard for my money, as you probably have, and I only invest in cash flow producing real estate. This is an asset I can leverage with good debt, the property covers all operational expenses, improvements, insurance, taxes, and debt while I patiently wait for the rents to increase and the value of the property then appreciates at which point we sell or refinance and own the property with no money invested.

I never deviate from this criteria. I invest my surplus cash into income-producing machines, in great locations, where the rent is less than the cost of home ownership, and I am buying at or below replacement cost. When I do invest, I buy very large deals, typically 200 to 1,000 units at a time, in markets with decades of projected job growth, and market demographics more likely to rent than own.

So, keep all this in mind while reading this book. You need to know how the author thinks when he/she gives you a strategy. I'm just sharing with you what has worked for me. I am sure there are other ways to make money investing but I can only share with you what has worked for me for 30 years, across seven states and through different economic conditions.

Also, as you are reading if you have questions all you have to do is call into our live show every Monday. If there is something you don't understand I will do my best to answer your questions. I want to help you get your money to work as hard for you and your family as you worked to earn it. It kills me to watch people lose money gambling on the stock market or simply ignoring their money, leaving equity in their home or giving it to a 401k to sit and decay for thirty years until they are old and can no longer use it.

I hope you enjoy reading this as much as I enjoyed writing it.

Let's go.

Chapter 1

How I Got Started - My First Mistake

•

REMEMBER, IF IT HAS ONE DOOR LIVE IN IT,
DON'T INVEST IN IT.

Chapter 1

How I Got Started - My First Mistake

The first real estate deal I bought was a $78,000 single-family home. I put $5,000 down and got a loan saying I would live in the house. By the time I closed the deal, I changed my mind (wink-wink) and rented the property to this nice girl and her sister. I thought I was so smart.

For the next 6 months I made $140 a month positive cash flow and it was looking like the investment was a great one. I did the math: $140 per month positive cash flow times 12 months equals $1,680 for the full first year representing a 33.6% return on my invested dollars, if I didn't incur any additional expenses and if the tenant stayed.

I was so excited and was experiencing illusions of one day becoming a real estate mogul. But, before I hit mogul status, 4 months later, reality set in. The sisters started calling every 3 days or so with some sort of complaint. First, it was the toilets, then termites, then roaches. A week or so later the neighbor called saying the girls hadn't mowed the lawn in 10 days. Then, I received more calls, this time about the electrical issues in the garage, the sewer backed up, and the garbage disposal malfunction. And that was all over the period of just a few months.

The time I was starting to spend on this one real estate deal was taking time away from my main job. I was a successful salesman in retail and I had to be there when the customer was. In retail, the customer demands your full attention and a great attitude, and you have to deliver on that to have any shot at success. Fixing stuff and handling tenant complaints was quickly wearing on me. I am the first to admit: I am good at solving problems and math, but I am terrible at fixing anything. So, every time something needed to be fixed, I called someone out, and plumbers, electricians, and service people aren't cheap. Not to mention, I wasn't able to pay attention to whether they were doing a good job or over-charging me. I didn't have time to get three bids, shop around, or check reviews. I was one person trying to handle my main job and this new real estate career. The dreaded *"Three T's"* of real estate were hitting me in the face: Tenants, termites, and toilets.

That was only the beginning of my issues. Then I was hit with the reality of *"one door renting."* One of the sisters called me to tell me what I feared the most, *"We are moving."* I was devastated and furious. I thought, *"How dare they move out, when I had done so much for them."* I was angry, disappointed, and discouraged, but more than anything, I was mostly scared.

It was November, and I knew I was going to have to make the payment to the bank without any income from the tenant. I hopefully thought, maybe I can get a tenant in next month, but I knew there was probably no way I would get a renter in before the next bank payment. I was worried about how long it would take to get a tenant during that time of the year.

Over the next 2 months, I would wipe out what I thought was going to be my full year of positive cash flow. Now, pay attention to this story because you don't want to repeat it.

It was November and going into Christmas Season. 'Tis the season to be merry, but not the season to find a tenant for a single-family home in cold, wet Houston, Texas. I had no advertising campaign and the property was hidden in a little neighborhood with almost no drive-by traffic. I had a full-time job that took a tremendous amount of attention and now I had an empty house, with no tenants, and a note due every month for the next 352 months.

I was planning on going to Mexico for a short vacation of warm sun and some fishing and that had to be cancelled because I had to get this place rented. On top of all that, I quickly realized I didn't know anything about the responsibility of being a landlord. I hadn't planned or prepared for any of this. I didn't know how to find tenants, how to maintain the property, manage the property or even how to place an ad. I hadn't fully understood the risk associated with renting one door.

I thought because I was only buying one unit, I had reduced my risk but, in truth, I had increased my risk because I was dependent upon one tenant. Remember, if it has one door live in it don't invest in it.

So, what did I do? I immediately put the single-family home on the market and did everything possible to sell it. By March it was sold, I licked my wounds and did the math. After fees to sell, I barely broke even and that is only because I managed (in my case mis-managed) the property myself. Technically, I only broke even because I refused to count any of the time I spent handling the property. The real estate brokers made more on the deal than I did and they only made $4,200. If it weren't for the speed at which I sold the property and the little bit of positive cash flow I did receive, I would have lost money.

My first deal wasn't a disaster, but it could have been. Fortunately, I paid attention to it and this experience changed my investing criteria forever. I realized quickly how little I understood about real estate investing and it reinforced all the warnings I had been given about the headaches of being a landlord. Rather than writing off the real estate investment vehicle as unviable, I elected to look at what I did wrong. I went back to study some of those earlier names I mentioned in the Introduction, who had created mega wealth with real estate, to see what I had done differently than what they had done.

> REMEMBER, IF IT HAS ONE DOOR LIVE IN IT, DON'T INVEST IN IT.

Immediately it was apparent to me. They all had created financial freedom with real estate and none of them were buying single-family homes, dependent upon one tenant. My deal had gone bad because I was dependent upon one tenant. Those real estate moguls were not dependent upon one tenant for cash flow. They could have 10% of their units vacant and still be cash flow positive, where if I lost one tenant, I was negative.

They built businesses that were based on renting many doors to many tenants, using the income to cover the expenses of operations, while they paid down debt and waited for appreciation.

Some people say they learn more from their mistakes than their successes; I highly suggest you don't try that in real estate. Learn from the mistakes of others. When investing money in anything, you cannot afford to learn from your own mistakes, you will end up broke! There is an old proverb that goes something like this: *"A fool learns from his own mistakes, the wise man learns from the mistakes of others."*

Most people lose money in real estate and blame the real estate, but I knew the real estate wasn't the problem. The way I was approaching the real estate was the problem. I had gone small and bought based on what I could afford. I was dependent upon one tenant and it cost me. I bought a small deal because I was scared to go bigger and it cost me. I had an immediate victory and quit learning and it cost me. I went in half-cocked in a hurry to brag about being a real estate owner and it cost me. And this is what most of us do on our first deals.

You see, I had bought what I could afford, based on the loan I could get and the money I had to put down. That limited me to only what I could afford and not necessarily the best investment.

I went back to the drawing board and spent the next 3 years learning everything I could about investing in real estate.

Just so you know my entire education has been on the ground walking deals, and without exaggeration, over the last 20 years I have walked tens of thousands of properties and interviewed hundreds of commercial real estate agents in Houston, San Diego, Tucson, Phoenix, Austin, Orlando, Tampa, Miami, Nashville, Savannah, Richmond and more.

In addition, I studied as many as 20 operating statements in a day and interviewed lenders from the biggest financial institutions in the world to learn the tricks of acquiring the best financing. When I was exhausted, I walked more properties and wore out brokers with more questions.

When I was first getting started, if I wasn't physically walking a property on the weekends, I was working my main job stashing cash.

I was committed to finding a GREAT deal, and knew I would need the cash, the courage, and the knowledge to pull the trigger. At the age of 31, I knew owning real estate was my financial freedom vehicle. I avoided investing in Keough's, IRA's, mutual funds, and individual stocks and bonds. I was keeping my powder dry for when I ran into my first deal, and while I did so, I was studying financial statements to understand why some deals worked and others didn't.

It would be 3 years before my first real apartment deal came along, but when it did, I was ready. I had the courage and the confidence and the cash. After looking at hundreds of properties and investing thousands of hours of studying, my first real deal was 48 units.

I knew the second I saw it I would buy it. I put the deal under contract the same day and was closed in under sixty days. My first real deal in the bag. I owned it for 4 years, and while I did, it paid for itself every month and provided me with positive cash flow and no headaches. I never took one phone call from one tenant about one problem, because I put a good manager in place. Four years later, I sold the property for an almost $4 million profit.

The belief that I would create wealth with real estate was validated with this first deal, and I knew one day I would get super rich with this vehicle. Since that first score, I have been buying apartments, repeating and perfecting how I buy deals, and studying more markets, financing, management, and all along the way, improving my connections within the real estate market in order to get better access to great deals.

Since that first deal, I have been through the savings and loan debacle, the internet bubble, and the housing collapse in 2008, and I have never lost money on an apartment deal. That original $350,000 investment in those 48 units was the seed capital for what is now almost 5,000 units worth almost $700 million and growing every day.

You can do this too, and you should. The real estate business is not super complicated but there is a lot to learn and also there are some myths (mistakes) you must avoid. I will cover this in more detail under *"mistakes to avoid,"* but for right now; A) you aren't going to do this with no money down, B) you can't manage the property yourself, C) small properties don't work, D) debt is critical to your purchase, and E) be willing to invest for the long term.

The other thing is, you either need to become an expert, or find and partner with one. Lastly, you owe it to your legacy and estate to invest in this asset class; in 20 years, you will have wished you did. The best days, months, and years of investing in cash flow positive apartments are in front of us, not behind us.

Chapter 2

The Different Kinds of Real Estate

•

"Homeownership is not a way to build wealth. It may be a place to save money - not make money."
- CNBC

Chapter 2

The Different Kinds of Real Estate

There are many kinds of real estate and I want to quickly touch on them, so when you are out doing your homework, you will understand why I like apartments so much.

Single-Family Residence or SFR – Is a type of property where a person should live, not where you should invest. You will hear a lot of people talk about a home as an investment, but in reality it is not an investment, it is liability. Houses were created for banks to profit, not for people to profit, and are mere traps where you and your family are forced to stay.

I understand you have to live somewhere and your argument that it is cheaper to own than rent, but this isn't true.

A study covered by CNBC suggests, *"Homeownership is not a way to build wealth. It may be a place to save money - not make money."*

When you consider property taxes, upkeep, roof repairs, air conditioning/heat repair, insurance, real estate fees and opportunity cost, not to mention your loss of mobility, a single-family home is a terrible investment.

> *"HOMEOWNERSHIP IS NOT*
> *A WAY TO BUILD WEALTH. IT MAY BE A PLACE TO*
> *SAVE MONEY - NOT MAKE MONEY."*
> - CNBC

Flipping or Wholesaling – This refers to taking a single-family home, improving it in some way and then reselling it, either before you close (sell the contract) or after you close. This, in reality, is not real estate investing but a form of speculating, or at best, another job whereby the investor buys a single-family home, improves it in some way and then sells it either to an end user, homeowner or to an investor who wants to rent it.

Every wholesaler I have ever interviewed ultimately wants to do what I do – own apartments that pay you every month for long periods of time. Wholesaling could be a good vehicle for getting the cash down payment to start buying apartments.

Single-Family Home Rental – This requires collecting single-family homes in your market and then renting them out, one at a time and keeping them for long periods of time. There was a rage across the country a decade ago where investors were collecting homes in their market, typically in low income neighborhoods, and the real estate investor would buy a home, and provide the tenant with an opportunity to lease with an option to purchase in the future. If they missed a payment they would remove the tenant from the home and do it again.

This is a combination of providing financing and renting, and in my opinion is predatory. This requires a hands-on owner and demands tremendous attention, making it very difficult to scale. You better be very tough to do this. While this can provide big percentage returns, you are simply trading time and stress for that return.

Another way to do this, is to get involved in government programs, whereby the landlord focuses on low income housing. In this arrangement, the landlord collects a portion of the rent money from the government (called *"Section 8"*) and a smaller amount from the tenant. In addition to requiring lots of your attention, the upside appreciation of these types of properties will be held down because the enterprise depends on the government for its revenue.

A relative of mine did this, collecting affordable housing where he lived, and over the years he collected three dozen or so single-family homes. Each deal had to be closed separately. My first apartment deal (48 units), required one closing and one loan and one address. I literally acquired more in one transaction than he had in a decade. This was one location to manage, not 48 different locations, and when I sold the property it was one sale, not dozens.

Duplexes & Fourplexes (not commercial) – This category of property type consists of two to four unit buildings, where the investor might live on the premises and rents the other units. This is the kind of investing most people start with, because they are investing on a budget rather than investing wisely.

While you can do this with less money down, it really is more like another job than it is investing. While everyone needs to start somewhere, I don't recommend this as the place.

Because the properties don't produce enough income, you will continue to be dependent upon your time and energy to make it work. And real estate values depend upon cash flow and location for its value in the future.

The loan you can get on these under four units deal are very attractive, normally requiring only 3% to 5% down with good credit. This is why so many people make this their first purchase – but it's a shortcut. People are lazy and go for the easy thing rather than the right thing.

The single-family homes, duplexes and fourplexes occupied by the owner are the first properties to be lost in foreclosure. Why? Because when the economy gets bad the investor doesn't have the money to continue to improve the property, and when one person moves out they are at least 25% vacant immediately. Remember that includes the owner renting one of the four units. So, now only 50% of the income of the property is covered. Two people move out and you are 75% vacant.

Commercial Property (5 units and above) – Just remember, while fewer units would appear easier to buy, they are harder to keep long term and much more difficult to make money on. Why? Because fewer units reduce your economies of scale and will never allow the property to produce enough income to warrant the work involved. What do Walmart, Amazon, Facebook, Coca-Cola, Sprint, and AT&T have in common? They have scale. They sell lots of units every day, not just a few.

In real estate, the fewer the doors the easier it may be to buy and the harder it is to make money. This is why I say the deck is stacked against the little guy and why I created Cardone Capital. The big guys don't spend time and energy buying little deals, they only buy the big stuff in great locations.

Do the math on eight doors and you can see why:

8 units x $800/month =	$6,400
$6,400 x 12 months =	$76,800
Expenses & Vacancy	$38,400
Cash Flow Before Debt	$38,400

That all assumes every unit is filled all year, you paid cash for the property, and have no debt. Depending on what you paid for this property and what you can sell it for (exit) determines whether you got a good deal.

If you paid $384,000 for the 8 units you are making 10%. If you paid $768,000 you are making 5%. This is the cash flow you receive while you wait to sell.

But the biggest problem here is scale. You can't scale this model and for real estate to create wealth for you, you must have these four ingredients:

1) Cash Flow
2) Time
3) Location
4) Scale

Eight units can only produce so much cash flow and will only be worth so much money to the next buyer.

If you figure expenses at 40% and vacancy at 10% and the deal now makes $38,400 a year before making any loan payments. Not bad, but there is one thing you missed; you have to manage this deal.

Now, before you think this is a good deal consider this: The expenses and vacancy are equal to $38,400 a year. How much does that allow for the property manager? If you pay the manager $38,000 a year, you have no money for the maintenance, repairs, taxes or to run the property. If you don't pay a manager, then you are working for $3,000 a month.

Figure you get a manager to run the deal in exchange to live at the property for free, and I assure you, you will not get the best tenants, your property will not get the best attention, and you will overpay on every bill. The average property management fee in the industry for a deal this size would be closer to 10% of the gross revenue, adding another $7,680 a year to your expenses. Any manager who works for $7,000 a year is worth nothing and just this penance cuts your return by almost a third.

Trust me, you need deals big enough to produce enough income to pay a good manager. If you pay the manager $4,000 a month ($48,000 a year), you lose money on this deal. If you don't pay $4,000 a month, you will be replacing managers all the time. And trust me, any manager that stays for less will be stealing from you. Trust me on this from personal experience.

The other issue on commercial loans is the banks require 25% to 35% down payment and good credit.

Any bank that does commercial real estate loans is going to measure four things to determine whether they will give you a loan:

1) The property.
2) Trailing 12 to 24 months of income.
3) Your credit score and net worth.
4) Your experience managing properties.

I know people with lots of money and perfect credit who have been denied commercial real estate loans because the bank felt they did not have the experience to manage property.

By the way, managing the property, requires a special temperament, a depth of knowledge, and special talents.

Ask yourself if you want to handle peoples calls, property tours, leases, and lease expirations. Do you have the time to build budgets, plan for rehabilitations, tenant turnovers, advertising, collections, complaints and more?

There is a saying in real estate that refers to *"The Three T's - Tenants, Termites, and Toilets,"* but really, it is much more than just those three things. Managing a property is like being in retail and not being paid a commission. The lower the rents the more difficult the property. The higher the rents, the more the tenant expects. You have to find the sweet spot in the middle and even then, you still better have a good location and a great manager.

Other Assets

Retail Properties – These are pieces of real estate like strip shopping centers and malls. The owner is renting to other business owners to operate their businesses. There are 28 million small businesses in America and most of them barely make any money. The investor of the strip center leases out to small businesses such as barbershops, restaurants, toy stores, clothiers, coffee shops, cosmetologists, tanners, yoga studios, and the like.

Coupon Clippers – This is where you are buying a property, building it out to suit a long-term lease from one tenant such as CVS, Starbucks, national restaurant chains, Sprint, Mattress Firm, banks, Walgreens, a grocery chain or the like. These big companies don't want to own the real estate. Their business isn't real estate, it is selling their product. They don't want the liability of the real estate on their financial statement to their investors, so they sign a long-term lease. This is where the real estate investor is again dependent upon the tenant doing well and continuing in business.

Here, you are very susceptible to economic conditions, but more concerning, is the disruptive changing technological culture we live in today. Consider you owned a property with a CVS anchor tenant. Just a year ago that was considered a very safe investment. The day Amazon announced they were going to get into the drug business, that investment became less desirable.

Office Buildings – Single or multi tenant building for the use of businesses renting space rather than owning. This can be a very capital intensive endeavor, requiring the owner to get a long term lease of 7 to 10 years, while managing capital to be invested for new tenants, referred to as *"tenant improvements."*

Property Classes

Before we leave this section, let's quickly cover the property classes. Property classifications were created to make it easier to communicate among investors and lenders to the quality and rating of the property amongst themselves. The class can refer to the property and the location.

A Class – Newest, shiniest asset and represent the highest quality building in the market. These are generally newer buildings under 15 years of age and contain many amenities catering to white-collar workers. Expect lower cap rates, around 2% to 4% on this asset.

This class of asset won't generate as much cash flow but has the ability to appreciate greatly. Class A Properties are great for preserving wealth, while investors wait patiently for appreciation. This investor has a reduced need for cash flow. * (I wish I would have bought more A Class over my career.) *

B Class – One step down from A and built within the last 20 years. This class caters to a mix of white and blue-collar workers and the property may show a bit of deferred maintenance, but overall, it has a nice mix of cash flow and potential appreciation. Look for returns on cash invested of 5% to 7%, before appreciation.

C Class – My first real estate broker defined C Properties as *"crap"* properties, but loved their ability to generate substantial cash flow. I tend to agree with his candid analysis.

These properties are usually 25+ years old and have deferred maintenance issues and are located in more difficult areas as well as needing big capital expenditure investments (new roof, interior remodels, etc.) to remain competitive. Look for cash on cash returns on cash invested of 8% and above on these properties, before appreciation.

D Class – The lowest class of properties usually located in cities with lower employment opportunities making it more difficult to collect the rent and more difficult to exit but greater cash flow for your trouble.

These properties are highly management intensive, and the tenant base is often difficult to deal with. Investors get lured into investing in these properties due to the low prices, but soon realize they got more than they bargained for.

The assignment of Property Classes A, B, C, & D are complete arbitraries and these descriptions are generalizations used more to communicate than anything. This is more opinion and less science and should only be used to give you an idea of the quality type and the location rating of the property.

Sometimes whether you are buying or selling impacts the property class used to describe the property. When I am buying the A Property, I see it as a B Property for negotiating purposes, and when I am selling, I described it as an A+.

Chapter 3

Why Apartments Are My Favorite Investment Vehicle

•

APARTMENTS ALLOW ORDINARY PEOPLE TO
PROTECT THEIR HARD-EARNED MONEY, AND
GET POSITIVE CASH FLOW, WHILE THEY WAIT
FOR APPRECIATION AND PAY DOWN DEBT. THIS,
I CALL "*THE ULTIMATE MULTIPLIER*" OR WHAT
OTHERS REFER TO AS LEVERAGE.

Chapter 3

Why Apartments Are My Favorite Investment Vehicle

Admittedly, I am a coward when it comes to investing and that is why I love apartments. Everything I have today I worked hard to get and I am extremely protective of it. Like you, I feel like I've worked really hard for my money and the last thing I want to do is blow it.

I was taught to have respect for money. My Dad taught me the value of money and stressed the need to be disciplined and responsible with it. I still remember the quarter my Dad trusted me with at the age of eight. I lost it when I was playing with it and will never forget my father saying, *"Don't play with money! Don't waste money! Don't lose money!"*

I know how hard a person must work to have money. I didn't come from money, I started from zero and I have a massive appreciation for anyone who can accumulate wealth. There is another level to money that most never learn, and that is the art of multiplying money.

This is the genius of money and why I love apartments so much. Apartments provide a safe place to keep money, receive income and multiply money. All the requirements necessary to create wealth are present in this investment vehicle.

Warren Buffet said, *"The first rule of investing is 'Don't lose money.' Rule number two is 'Don't forget rule number one.'"*

He's also said, *"Never invest in anything with the idea it's ok to lose money."* These simple concepts have shaped my commitment to apartments as the best investment for me.

So, let's see if apartments pass Warren Buffett's test (*"Don't lose money."*) When you buy an apartment building that produces positive cash flow in excess of the cost to manage, will that property be there tomorrow and in the future?

We all know the value of money goes down over time (depreciates) and most people would agree that real assets, property, in good locations will go up in value over time. This passes Warren Buffett's first two rules.

Now, if we look at Warren's next criteria, he buys companies that produce cash flow. He buys Coca-Cola, See's Candies, Burlington Railroads, Wells Fargo, and now Apple. Why? These companies produce positive cash flow.

Contrary to popular belief, Warren Buffet is not an investor in stocks, he invests in companies that are indestructible, produce dependable cash flow, and which will increase (appreciate) in value over time due to their ability to produce cash flow. Warren Buffet uses a depreciating asset (cash) to buy appreciating companies that produce more cash.

Now, understand that most of us cannot take major positions in Coca-Cola or Wells Fargo, but we can buy apartments.

Here are the four main reasons I love apartments:

1) They're real assets, not paper, and they can't be easily replaced.

2) They produce positive cash flow.

3) Apartments appreciate when rents rise– the Multiplier.

4) Leverage of debt to increase your position.

Let me explain by using an example: I am buying an apartment building in Orlando, Florida; let's see if it stands the test of the four main reasons I like apartments.

This property is 240 units, in a great location across from the Ritz-Carlton Hotel, with great street frontage, is 95% occupied, and produces a positive cash flow in the first month of ownership of 8% annualized.

First Rule - Cannot be easily replaced – Don't lose money. Short of some worldwide devastation, this property will not suddenly disappear and is built to last hundreds of years. No technology can suddenly replace it. The property is in a great location where there are lots of good jobs and where people want to live.

Second Rule - Produce positive cash flow – The property produces 5% to 8% positive cash flow per year, based on current operations. I will put $15 million down to buy the $50 million property, which should pay investors at Cardone Capital from $900,000 to $1,200,000 per year.

Third Rule - Appreciation: The Multiplier – Now, this is very important. Our target for all our investments is to sell the property, at some time in the future, where we make a minimum of 100% on our investment, in addition to the cash flow.

Fourth Rule - Leverage: The Ultimate Multiplier – The ultimate multiplier is the fact that we can use one dollar and buy four. What investment allows you to invest $1 million and own $4 million in assets? Add to that: these are real assets that can't be easily replaced or lost (1), plus cash flow (2), meaning we are paid to wait for appreciation (3).

So, we receive cash flow on the down payment, and waited for the entire $4 million to appreciate; this is the ultimate multiplier combining leverage and appreciation with cash flow.

So, at what price would I need to sell this $50 million property for us make 100% on our money? At first glance, you would think I need to sell for $100 million to make 100%, but in reality, because we used leverage (debt) I only have to sell it for $65 million to accomplish our 100% target. Investors paid $15 million to buy the property, not $50 million, as I was able to leverage my relationships with lenders and get a great loan.

So, lets say it takes me 10 years to accomplish this to see if it is even reasonable.

1) Will the property still be there in 10 years? 99.99% chance it will and insurance covers the .01%. Can it be easily replaced? It can't be destroyed and it will cost more to build in 2028.

2) Positive cash flow of just 6% a year (very conservative) will produce $900,000 ($15 million x 6%) in free cash flow to investors and this assumes current cash flow percentages without rent growth. Remember, this is for 10 years, which represents 60% of our down payment.

3) Appreciation – The future value of apartments, unlike homes, is determined based on the future value of the rent. The current rents on the property are $1,500, is it possible that the rents in 2028 would be conservatively closer to $2,000 or more? This increase in the rents of only $500 ($50 a year) will increase the value of the property because the income of the property has increased.

4) Leverage – Remember, this is the ultimate multiplier. We paid $15 million for an asset worth

$50 million. If it only goes up in value by $15 million, and sells for $65 million (easy to imagine) we've made 100% on our money. Our capital invested doubled without the asset doubling. Get it?

And this brings me to the calculation of your exit formula. If you don't know how to calculate this, you will be stuck in the deal forever. When I buy a deal, I have an idea of what I am going to sell it for and even who the likely buyer might be.

It seems impossible to predict the future but in reality, if you can't calculate the exit, future value, and possible buyer, you shouldn't buy the deal.

Rents will determine future value of your asset and the ability for someone to pay you a profit going forward. This is another reason why I love this asset class so much.

The EXIT Formula (future value calculation)

To properly calculate the exit of your purchase you have must know how to calculate future values. The only way the property will be worth more money is because it produces more NOI. The NOI can only be increased because the rents increased greater than the cost to operate.

Let me use the example of the 240 units I recently bought. Assuming, over the next five to ten years I can increase the rents only $50 per month, which by the way, only means I need to increase rents 3% per year. Over five years that would be a 30+% increase on the current rent of $1500. Easy for me to assume the rents might be $2000 a month in 2028.

So, this is how future value would be figured:

> 240 units
>
> x $500 (rent increase)
>
> x 12 (months)
>
> x 95% (occupied)
>
> = NOI increase of $1,368,000

Increase in Value = $22,800,000 (NOI/6% Cap Rate).

Remember, we bought this deal with $15,000,000 and financed $35,000,000. When we bought it, the property was doing 5% to 8% cash flow after all expenses and debt. In 2028, if the rents increase by only $50 per year, this means I could sell the property for $72,800,000 based on the same cap rate or even a little higher cap rate in 2028.

So, what did we make on the deal?

1) Return of Capital	$15,000,000
2) Cash Flow	$9,000,000
	($900,000/year x 10 year)
3) Profit	$22,800,000

It would appear that our $15 million investment is now worth $46,800,000, an increase of 312%.

BOOM!

Since this might be confusing, take a few moments and go back over the math. I know you don't believe these kinds of returns are possible because you have never been in deals that do this. See why I am going to change the real estate investing models with Cardone Capital?

By the way, I have delivered these kinds of returns on over 30 different deals in 7 different states.

While I would never promise every deal can or will achieve these kinds of returns, I can tell you I put my money where my beliefs are. Almost 95% of my net worth is invested in the types of real estate deals I am describing in this book or that you will see at CardoneCapital.com

When I buy a property at Cardone Capital, I purchase it with my funds, and then let other investors in after the fact. The seller of the property knows I am buying their deal and assured of closing because my funds and credit ability are backing the purchase, not whether investors come in with me or not. I am the one signing on the loan and promising the $35 million loan gets paid back, not another group, and I don't have to go to anyone for approval, which gives the seller more certainty. This is how you get the great deals.

You see, my Dad taught me how to work hard, respect money, save the money I made, and not buy stupid stuff with it, unfortunately, he did not live long enough to teach me how to multiply money. I had to learn that on my own and it took me years to figure out the model.

Years ago, your parents and grandparents put their money in the bank and earned 8% to 10%. These rates have not existed for 20 years and won't in the future so you must find other ways to multiply money. You are losing money while it sits in checking and money market accounts. The average bank pays less than ½ of 1% on your money today. The average return on our apartment projects suggest a 15% return which is 30X what you earn at the bank or Fidelity or Merrill.

In my last best seller, *The Millionaire Booklet*, I write there are three things you must learn about money to create wealth:

1) How to get it,
2) How to keep it, and
3) How to multiply it.

You must learn to multiply your money and apartments are one of the best vehicles for doing this. Apartments allow ordinary people to protect their hard-earned money, and get positive cash flow, while they wait for appreciation and pay down debt. This, I called *"The Ultimate Multiplier"* or what others refer to as leverage.

Let's look at my first apartment deal, so you can learn from what I did right. My first apartment deal made me $4 million in 39 months, so clearly, I did something right. The real success of this deal was done before I even bought the deal, by knowing the market so well that when I stumbled across the deal, I knew it was a steal. I had cash ready and I knew enough about the market to have the confidence to move with speed and certainty before someone else did.

> APARTMENTS ALLOW ORDINARY PEOPLE TO PROTECT THEIR HARD-EARNED MONEY, AND GET POSITIVE CASH FLOW, WHILE THEY WAIT FOR APPRECIATION AND PAY DOWN DEBT. THIS, I CALLED *"THE ULTIMATE MULTIPLIER"* OR WHAT OTHERS REFER TO AS LEVERAGE.

Most investors miss great deals because they aren't sure, and by the time they are ready, someone else owns it. Just consider how many great deals you have already missed because you weren't sure.

I looked at hundreds of deals in the market before I bought my first deal. Over my career, I have looked at hundreds of thousands of apartments, that's right, hundreds of thousands. I know the moment I walk on a property whether I will buy it or not. With my first deal, I knew within seconds it was a great deal and that I could trust it to provide me positive cash flow in all economic environments, and appreciation in the future.

It was in the right location, convenient to jobs, highways, easily visible from street traffic, more affordable than the homes in the surrounding neighborhoods, priced below replacement cost, in a market with high barriers to entry, probably a B Class product in a B Class neighborhood and it felt good with great street presence. Until you are able to spot these indicators, you are not ready to invest on your own.

I found out in due diligence, management wasn't really paying attention; the seller was tired, and I was able to buy the property for less than the cost to build it. This is referred to as "*replacement cost.*" Because of its location in the country, the cost to build new product, as well as the political environment, this created barriers to entry preventing new competition (new construction), that might underprice my rents and steal my tenants. If anyone could build next door, it would be a much higher price, and because their cost would be higher, they would be forced to rent at higher rates and the competition would help me, not hurt me.

Because I had done extensive homework on the market, had my down payment ready to go, and banks were comfortable providing me with financing, the seller took me seriously and immediately accepted my offer.

I got the deal under contract (an art in and of itself) and closed the deal thirty days later. A quick close almost always means you can buy a deal for a discount.

My first deal wasn't just bought at a discount, it was a steal. 48 units for $1,950,000, and I put $350,000 down. I financed the difference and the rents from the properties paid all the expenses, management fees, utilities, repairs, insurance, taxes, the loan, and I still had money left over to pay myself every month for the entire time I owned it.

Remember the first rule, don't lose money? Remember, I want cash flow while I wait and I want it every month. I have also insisted this for our investors at Cardone Capital.

It is not enough for me to not lose money or wait long into the future for a profit. My investors and I deserve to be paid monthly on our invested capital, as long as the property has positive cash flow.

The right apartments, in the right location, bought at the right time, at the right price, should provide investors with consistent positive cash flow, while we wait for rents to go up and the loan amount to be paid down and appreciation to take place.

Leverage Explained

Real Estate Riddle:

> If you and I buy a $20 million property with $5 million down and it cash flows at 10% a year what did the property cost us?

Answer:

> The $20 million property cost us nothing.
>
> The $5 million less the cash flow of the 10% per year for 10 years ($500,000 a year) means our original investment is returned in 10 years. Now, we literally own the property with no cash.

Real Estate Riddle:

> If we buy a $20 million property with $5 million down and it does <u>not</u> cash flow what did it cost us?

Answer:

> $5 million.

This is leverage.

As an investor, you want to get your down payment back as fast as possible. I look at cash flow as a way to reimburse myself over time for the money I put down, ensuring at some point in the future, me and the investors no longer have money in the deal.

That's right, my goal is to own a deal with no cash in it, then we wait to sell for a profit.

Now, I want to share with you the power of cash flow, to simplify your investing and ensure the property is a good investment.

Cardone Cash Flow Formulas for
Zero Cash In Calculation

I am going to share with you a simple calculation to figure out how long it takes to get your investment back at different cash flow levels. This is how it works: divide 100% by the annual cash flow to determine how many years it takes to get your down payment back.

How do you lose money if you're original money has been returned?

Now, stay with me here, what are the chances the rents will be slightly higher in 5 years than they are today? As the rents go up, the property will produce more cash flow to investors and this is what causes appreciation. The apartment's value is not determined by comparables like a house is. The apartment's value is determined by the rents and the cash flow produced by the property.

In the example above, I showed a never changing cash flow which would be almost impossible considering the upward trajectory of rents over the last 30 years.

Let's assume the cash flow is the same every year. Use the formula below to determine how long it takes to return your original investment. 100% divided by the percent of cash flow = years to have investment returned.

Cardone Cash Flow Formulas for Zero Cash In Calculation		
6% per year	100% / 6%	16.7-years
10% per year	100% / 10%	10 years
15% per year	100% / 15%	6.7 years
20% per year	100% / 20%	5 years (definitely doable)

At this point, we haven't even considered things like forced appreciation, property enhancements, upgrades, debt pay down, depreciation, and tax benefits.

All I am talking about here is CASH FLOW.

Why do I believe apartments are the best investment available over the next 30 years?

1) Demographics heavily suggest people are more interested in using (renting) than owning. You can see this everywhere. Home ownership is at the lowest level in 40 years. The leasing of automobiles, once frowned upon, is at the highest level ever.

2) 80+ million aging baby boomers are more likely to move into rentals in the future, than to buy a new home.

3) Millennials are having families later than any time in history and delaying the home purchase and are more likely to rent.

4) Affordability of home ownership continues to get out of reach for most Americans due to flat wages, no savings and poor credit.

5) The fantasy of home ownership as *"The American Dream"* was scathed in 2008 when millions of Americans lost their homes.

6) America has experienced 26 years of flat wages nationwide and this will continue as we move into automation and higher unemployment in the future.

7) Rental property has outperformed stocks, bonds, and cash over the last 20 years.

8) There is a shortage of affordable housing stock in almost every growing city in America.

9) New housing product cannot be built affordably, putting continued upward pressure on rents.

10) Leverage – Unlike stocks, bonds, ETFs and mutual funds, the bank will lend you 65% to 75% of the purchase.

Consider this: Bank of America will not lend you money to invest in Bank of America stock, but they will lend you money to buy an apartment building.

11) Cash Flow – Apartments bought correctly will provide positive cash flow monthly, unlike other investment vehicles.

12) Debt Pay Down – The income of the property, less expenses, should provide enough Net Operating Income (NOI) to pay the principal debt down.

13) Tax Benefits – All interest, expenses, maintenance, repairs and depreciation, are tax-deductible items.

14) Capital Gains – Properties held longer than 1 year are taxed at lower rates than personal income.

15) New tax laws – Cash flow produced from real estate is taxed at the lower rates.

16) Apartments are real investments – Unlike most of what is offered by Wall Street, apartments are real property, with real tenants paying real money, who have a real reason to continue to do so.

Buy the right deal, at the right time, in the right location that has the right size to it and as long as you take care of the property, and there is no urgent need to sell you are almost guaranteed to see appreciation in the future.

How To Create Wealth Investing In Real Estate • CardoneCapital.com

Chapter 4

The Three Ways to Invest in Apartments

•

REMEMBER THIS RULE: IF THE DEAL IS
EASY TO GET, IT PROBABLY ISN'T ANY GOOD,
AND THE MORE INTEREST IN THE DEAL,
THE MORE VALUE IT WILL HAVE
TO THE NEXT SET OF BUYERS.

Chapter 4

The Three Ways to Invest in Apartments

There are basically three ways to invest in apartments:

1) Do It Yourself
2) REIT (Real Estate Investment Trust)
3) Partnership

1) Do It Yourself – Buying apartments on your own is for a much smaller number of people than you would think, but you won't know that until you read the next chapter on mistakes.

The mistakes you will make in real estate are not as obvious as you might think, and most all of them are made because people go it alone. However, the biggest mistake of all, is to never buy income producing real estate at all.

This is what you will need to do if you are going it alone:

1) Find a deal
2) Negotiate the terms
3) Set up an LLC
4) Get a loan
5) Close the deal
6) Find tenants
7) Turn units
8) Manage the property
9) Rehab the property
10) Provide reports to the bank
11) Take phone calls from existing and prospective tenants
12) Fix the property.

Of all things on that list, the hardest part of investing in apartments isn't the tenants, the termites, and the toilets, it's in finding the right deal. Finding the deal (on-market or off-market) is the most difficult part of buying apartments. Sometimes just getting the seller or broker to take you seriously is difficult.

I remember when I told my Mom I was going to start buying apartments and she said to me, *"People are going to be calling you at all times of the night."* I thought to myself, *"No one is calling me; I am buying deals big enough whereby the property can afford a management team."*

On most of our properties the tenants don't know the names of our investors as the property is under an LLC ownership, not our personal names. When a tenant calls for assistance, he or she gets a well paid manager who is well trained on how to resolve the tenants issues. No one calls me or the investors, because the property produces enough income to pay a great manager to deliver a great experience (more about this in the chapter on mistakes).

Finding deals would seem to be the easiest part when buying apartments, but in reality, finding the deal is the most difficult task of all. Remember this rule: if the deal is easy to get, it probably isn't any good, and the more interest in the deal, the more value it will have to the next set of buyers.

I have bought deals before just because of the amount of interest, knowing I could sell it the next day if I wanted to. I recently bought a 500 unit deal for Cardone Capital and within 2 months of closing I was offered an $11 million profit.

> REMEMBER THIS RULE: IF THE DEAL IS EASY TO GET, IT PROBABLY ISN'T ANY GOOD, AND THE MORE INTEREST IN THE DEAL, THE MORE VALUE IT WILL HAVE TO THE NEXT SET OF BUYERS.

You want there to be competition on every deal you buy. I will even tell you this, having to pay more to get a deal is a good sign of the value of the deal. The old adage, *"Buy low and sell high"* sounds good, but it will not be your best strategy with apartments. Warren Buffet says, *"Far better to buy a wonderful company at a fair price than buy a fair company at a wonderful price."*

2) REIT – Real Estate Investment Trust. This is like buying stock or paper and not investing directly into the real estate. This is great for those who want the cash flow yield but don't kid yourself this is <u>not</u> a real estate investment. And in fact the IRS does not allow owners in a REIT any of the great tax advantages offered to owners of real estate.

3) Partnership – This is where you either create a partnership or become an investing partner with other professional real estate investors who are investing in real estate.

A) Create your own partnership and do all the work. You find the deal, negotiate and manage it, and raise funds from friends and family. This is a lot of work for you and is a full time job. Now, you aren't just buying deals and managing them, you also have to do fundraising.

Typically, you will pay them 6% to 10% on their investment, unless you have to get hard money loans that can cost 12% to 20% and then do some kind of split on the profits above those payouts.

B) Syndicator. You invest money with a professional real estate investor who is basically doing (A) above and he raises money from others to buy and manage deals. The syndicator makes most of his money from fees. While the syndicator will also benefit from selling at a profit, the person investing in this model is typically less interested in the upside profit.

The downside of this model is, the syndicator has to sell out of the property at a certain date in the future. While this is sold as a benefit to the investors it is actually a detriment in bad markets.

C) Partner on a Profit Sharing / Cash Flow Formula. This is what we do at Cardone Capital. This model is different from other investment models as it makes extraordinary deals available to ordinary investors.

Investors partner with me on real estate deals experiencing all the benefits of real estate and ride as passive investors, experiencing all the upside of investing and none of the headaches. I will tell you more about this in the last chapter.

Regardless of the ways you elect to get involved, if you learn the investing game, avoid the mistakes, do what I say, and never find yourself forced to sell in bad markets: you will make money.

Remember, there is a shortage of larger, affordable apartment complexes in America and this will continue to reveal itself over the next 30 years. Look around your city and count the number of 300 unit complexes that offer affordable rents.

This shortage will make the large, affordable, quality apartment complexes more and more valuable over time. As we move into the future, rents will rise in markets where there is job growth. Also, as we move into the future, inflation increases the cost to build, thus making it more difficult to build affordable apartments.

What you should know by now from reading this is: you must figure out how to get yourself in bigger deals. Small deals don't work.

I have a buddy who owns 1,000 units on his own. I showed him some of the deals we are buying at Cardone Capital and he wrote me a check for $1.5 million on the spot. He said, *"I can't get these bigger deals, and the bigger deals are where the big returns are."*

I will show you how, and more importantly, I will show you why you don't want to do anything other than the bigger deals.

Chapter 5

Mistakes to Avoid When Investing in Apartments

•

CHEAPER IS NOT BETTER. I HAVE MADE MY BEST
DEALS, AND BEST RETURNS, ON BUYING HIGH
AND SELLING HIGHER.

Chapter 5

Mistakes to Avoid When Investing in Apartments

I have made so many mistakes in real estate. The one mistake I have not made is losing money. 25 years, over $700 million in transactions, and I have never lost money on an apartment deal, but I have made many mistakes.

My first deal was a mistake because it was single-family and relied on one tenant. I broke even on that deal, and only because I didn't account for the time I invested in managing and getting rid of it. If I included all my time, it was a loser.

Here is a list of mistakes you want to avoid when investing. I tried to write them in the order of importance.

Mistakes Made When Investing in Apartments:

1) Not Investing – Not investing in this asset class is the ultimate, biggest mistake you will make with your finances. While it may seem difficult right now, due to limited funds, credit, experience and confidence, you owe it to yourself to figure this out.

Whether you buy deals on your own, or with me, get involved. When done right, apartments can produce passive income for generations and mind boggling returns, without the risks of other investments.

2) Buying Too Small – Anything under 16 units will not produce enough free cash flow to warrant doing the deal. 2 units, 4 units, 6 units, and 8 units are not enough scale to make sense of the deal, unless you are buying to merely flip the property, but now you are speculating not investing.

3) Single-Family Home Rentals – This is an issue because you are dependent upon one tenant. Never invest in one door. Live where there is one door and own where there are many.

Single-family homes are bad investments for the most part and have proven to be for the last 30 years, earning about 1% per year when adjusted for inflation. Millions of people found this out in 2008 when they lost their homes.

Single-family homes are terrible investments for rental income but they are easy to purchase. Remember, easy to purchase means hard to keep.

4) Using Too Much Debt – Using too much debt will resort in the property being unable to service the debt at some point in the economic cycle. If you can buy it with 95% financing, that means other people can too, and the more people, the fewer barriers to purchase, the less valuable the property will be in the future.

I watched so many real estate guys lose everything in 2008 because they over-leveraged and speculated. I only use 50% to 75% debt on my deals. So, if a deal is $50 million, I expect to put down up to $25 million to buy the deal.

This kind of commitment to capital investment excludes a lot of buyers and becomes a built-in barrier to entry. This is what the big guys know that little investors don't and why the big guys get the great deals and the little guys get the left overs.

This is the simple economics of supply and demand. I now own something most people can't buy which will make this asset more valuable in 5 to 10 years, or more, when I go to sell. Now, that being said, too much money down may mean the product is overpriced.

At Cardone Capital we have created relationships with the largest lenders in the world and receive debt terms not available to the public at large. Know what you are doing when it comes to picking your debt partner. By the way, you need a number of different lenders for different asset classes and different cycles. Never rely on one lender, the debt is a critical part of your investment and developing relationships with lenders is vital.

I can't tell you how many times a seller has asked me, *"Have you ever assumed a Fannie Mae or Freddie Mac loan?"* The seller wants to know if you can get financing done and that your equity is ready.

5) Buying on Price and Cap Rate – If you only buy deals based on the lowest prices or the highest cap rates, you will never get great deals. The great deals always come at a premium price and a lower cap rate. As crazy as it seems, my best deals have been the ones I paid the most for.

The old adage, *"Buy low and sell high"* is true, until it's not. I have made my best deals, and best returns, on buying high and selling higher.

The lowest price in apartments is not an indication of a great deal. It is an indication that something is wrong. I can buy property at cheaper prices and higher cap rates in suburban Detroit than I can in the Galleria of Houston.

CHEAPER IS NOT BETTER. I HAVE MADE MY BEST DEALS, AND BEST RETURNS, ON BUYING HIGH AND SELLING HIGHER.

I once bought a deal in Austin, paid the asking price, didn't negotiate a penny, and closed quickly. I knew when I bought it someone else would pay me more. I sold the deal for 115% return in 6 months.

I knew there was a trend for tech companies to move to Austin at the time, and knew it was only a matter of time before someone paid me a profit. I just miscalculated how soon it would be. I bought the deal, closed on it, got great financing, and spent $5,000 resurfacing the parking lot when a buyer came along and offered me $4 million more than I paid. I put $4 million down and he gave me $8 million to go away.

I was also the top bidder, and paid the highest price, on a portfolio in Florida. This was my first purchase in the state and no one knew me, so I had to pay more to get the deal. There were 38 other groups bidding on the deal. Why was I willing to pay the most? The amount of interest on the deal led me to believe I could later sell the portfolio to one of the other 38 who wouldn't stretch to get the property.

I paid $58 million for the portfolio. What does it matter if I overpaid by $100,000 or even $500,000? If you are going to be in a deal for 5 to 10 years $500,000 should not change your opinion of the deal. A great deal is not determined by the price you pay, but rather, the price the next guy is willing to pay.

> A GREAT DEAL IS NOT DETERMINED
> BY THE PRICE YOU PAY...

I have owned that deal for 5 years now. It pays me an average of 26% cash on cash and I could fire sell the portfolio for $150 million. By the way, I guarantee you one of the 38 who bid against me 5 years ago would try to buy it from me today at the higher price.

Talk about a good deal for the investors. My sister, one of the first investors in Cardone Capital, who is 10 years older than me and retired, has made more money from this one investment than she made from all her previous jobs and investments combined!

Every month for the last 5 years, she has received a check from her investment twice the size of any salary from any position she held as an executive assistant to oil executives. This was a game changer for her and provided her with an opportunity she could never do on her own. But she has also been a good investor, positive, patient and believes in what we are doing at Cardone Capital.

When you are buying deals no one else is competing on, you have to wonder what's wrong. If no one else will eat it, you might want to leave it alone. Why does no one else want this? Is everyone wrong but you? That could be the case by the way. Maybe you see or know something no one else can see or know. This has happened where I was the first to see the value in a market, a location or an opportunity.

Also, too much action should be a warning. You have probably heard me say, *"Cranes in the air: Beware."* When the builders start building new apartments in the market you will be smart to become extremely cautious.

Builders, for the most part, are not great investors; they are great builders, most of which, at some point, go broke. They tend to lose all the money they made in the deals they built in the last few they should not have built.

New apartments serve as competition for existing product. There is, however, a time in the market where the building stops and will then stay dormant for too many years in the future, creating another opportunity for the smart investor.

That is one of the reasons I am so excited about Houston at this time. They overbuilt and the next response by builders and investors will be to avoid that market and wait until the new apartments are absorbed (rented).

I will go there early, find great opportunities and sit and wait for those investors to come back when they realize there isn't enough new product because the builders all abandoned the market. This takes patience, foresight and the ability to move from market to market, which the small investor cannot do.

6) Not Using a Broker – Trying to buy the deal without a commercial broker is a pure rookie mistake. The broker is your friend in this game. I use a broker on every deal and prefer to only use the listing broker and hope he/she makes a bunch of money on the deal.

I recently bought a deal that was not on the market (off- market) and I had a broker in another city represent my offer only because he knew the seller. I paid him $250,000 to do this for me when I could have probably done it for myself. Why?

Because, I need a buffer between me and the seller. We did the deal and I assumed an unbelievable loan of $63 million on 500+ units in the heart of one of America's great cities. 60 yards away is Amazon's office, Whole Foods, Starbucks is walking distance, there are $800,000 townhomes across the street and you have to drive past $2 million homes to get to the property where the average tenant is a professional making five times what they pay in rent. (Income to rent ratio is a very important metric.)

I think my partners and I will hold this asset and sell it for double what we paid for the entire deal, returning 400% to the investors in a deal that cash flows. If I am going to make $60 million on a project, I don't worry about paying a broker $250,000 because he helps me secure the deal. Pay the broker and know them all and make sure they like you.

7) **Not Looking at Enough Deals** – I look at 100 deals to buy one, so unless you are smarter than me or luckier than me, be prepared to look at that many deals.

I have friends who are financially very successful and could buy deals on their own but quickly realize they don't have time to look at enough deals to know the right deal. Because they are successful they have their hands full operating their successful businesses and their families.

To find great deals, you have to be in the market everyday looking at deals, sometimes it takes years before the market is even ready to invest in. I have bought and sold deals in 7 states now and to buy deals in just your local market takes more energy, time and resources than you can imagine. Just getting brokers to call you back, is an art.

To buy a deal in a market outside of where you live requires trips, hotels, nights away from home, appointments, and planning. The deals we are closing right now are both monsters outside of where I live, and were the result of looking at over 6,000 units.

Interestingly enough, neither deal was something we went to look at, but were both the result of either stumbling upon a location or developing a relationship with a broker on other deals. The one we stumbled upon, and I immediately knew I would buy, was not even on the market. I would not have found this jewel had I not been actively looking in the market.

My wealthy friends who partner with me on deals do so because they simply don't have the time to look at the number of deals we look at. They can also do bigger deals with me than they could on their own and tap into the great financing we have access to.

One of the reasons I bought my jet a few years ago was so that I could fly into markets at a moment's notice and look at deals.

Again, my formula requires we use tremendous discipline and research, looking at some 100+ deals for each one we close. For that reason, other real estate professionals invest with me at Cardone Capital because of the number of deals we see. My social media presence hasn't hurt in helping us find deals either.

If you watched the 2017 World Series you noticed I was sitting in the front row of Game 7. Yes, it was the best seat in the house. Location matters in real estate and you want to be seen. I wasn't doing that to show off but because I wanted to get the attention of every major commercial broker controlling apartments in Houston, Texas.

Remember, the Astros won the World Series, and I bought the deal of the year. Investing in real estate the right way is a full-time job; it takes money, energy, effort, relationship building, and anyone that tells you it doesn't isn't doing their due diligence.

8) Unable to Move to Other Markets – I have bought in eight different markets. I knew when I started I would only be able to do so much in the one market where I lived.

In the beginning, as a real estate investor you should stay local. But, what if where you live the market sucks or is already overbuilt or even dying? People in Canada for instance, don't have a lot of apartments to buy. There is very little of this stock, so not a lot of trading going on.

People in European countries don't have this asset class to invest in the way we do in America.

Remember, not everyone makes money in real estate because not all markets are good. If you had invested anywhere around Detroit in the last 20 years, you had dead money unless you were in downtown where money recently started being invested; and that play is still up in the air as to whether it will work or not.

I AM NOT A SPECULATOR;
I AM AN INVESTOR...

Don't speculate; invest in sure things. I am not a speculator; I am an investor, and that means, at some point, I'll have to move to markets outside of where I'm living and raising my kids. To move outside means you will need a team to research other markets, find deals in those markets, and then manage the property there.

9) Not Knowing the Market – Know your market completely. You need to know every sale, every comp, every rental, what properties are under-rented, what properties are over-leveraged, what that property sold for in the last cycle, the vacancy in your market, and the cost of every expense. Insurance, utilities, management fees, the cost to turn, how long it takes to turn, the cost to advertise, which ads work, foot traffic, closing ratios, trailing 12 months of operation, and then you need to know and have relationships with the top 3 controlling brokers in the market to find the best apartment stock in the market.

Look, I am not trying to scare you here, but there are so many courses out there suggesting real estate is easy when, in truth, there is a lot to know. There are a number of tools you might want to invest in, like Real Capital Analytics, which gives you the selling and financing history of a property. Axiometrics provides you with rent comps and Co-Star breaks down property detail information, rent comparable and sales history.

These programs can cost up to $20,000 a year for your local market and can give you a lot of intel. LoopNet is free and is basically for amateurs (Loopsters), but can be great source to find brokers. The top brokers don't typically list their properties on LoopNet but only on their sites. When you call a broker, don't even mention you saw it on LoopNet, you will lose credibility.

10) Financing – You need debt (financing) arms (not one) that will provide you with great terms and the confidence that you can close the deal. Buying apartments without using debt makes no sense. If it wasn't for the debt, I wouldn't be able to do the big deals and max out returns.

On my first deal, I had to go to 3 lenders and the first 2 told me no. I took the *"No's"* personally, only to find out later these banks didn't lend on apartments and that is why they told me no. But, the banks almost never say, *"We aren't lending on apartments at this time."* They will give you some other lame reason why they won't do the deal.

You need to know who is lending on deals, and who is not, and you also need to know their underwriting criteria for approving the loan. Understanding the debt component is vital to deal-making as it will provide you with the confidence in your financing to give the seller assurance you can close the deal.

I have been borrowing money and creating relationships with the biggest apartment lenders in the world for 30 years. Fannie Mae, Freddie Mac, life insurance companies, and banks, all know me now, and assist me in understanding and underwriting my deals. They are partners with me in helping me make my deals work. The lender is not an adversary, it's your partner. I did not understand this early on.

THE LENDER IS NOT AN ADVERSARY, IT'S YOUR PARTNER.

I have borrowed some $550 million dollars from lenders, all of which, at some point in the future, is being paid down by the operations of the apartments. In many cases, the debt I use on a deal can be worth more than the deal itself, but I will save that for another book.

11) Not Buying Through All Cycles – To play the real estate game, you cannot just buy at the bottom. You must be able to buy at the bottom, the middle, and yes, even at the top. As long as you have enough cash flow, the property will make a new top as long as you are in the right market and have cash flow to carry you through economic cycles.

"Why not just wait until the bottom?" I hear this all the time. If you aren't buying through all the cycles, you won't buy any of them. The brokers won't know you and no one will take you seriously if you are just coming in when there is *"Blood in the streets."*

When the market is bad, the seller and broker become even more concerned about the ability of the buyer to close. The highest price does not get the best deals in bad markets; trust and confidence to close get the deals. Whoever has the most confidence to close gets the great deals. If they don't know you, they won't close with you.

In summary, buy apartments. Don't go small, don't buy the junk, buy the best product in the market place, make sure you have cash flow, and take care of the property and the tenants. When you find that deal: move fast.

Chapter 6

Your First Deal

•

PAY ATTENTION TO THIS RECIPE
AND YOUR FIRST DEAL HAS A
BETTER CHANCE OF BEING A WINNER.

Chapter 6

Your First Deal

Let me show you what your first deal should look like, so you have specific criteria and don't waste time on deals that won't be good for you. Pay attention to this recipe and your first deal has a better chance of being a winner.

Before I walk you through the criteria of your first deal, let me give you some basic terms you will need to get accustomed to hearing and using to understand a financial statement.

Gross Rental Income – This is the total possible income if every unit is rented at the full price. This figure is used by the broker and is almost meaningless.

Effective Gross Income – This is the amount of rental income actually collected and is a very important number.

Other Income – This would include collections from utility reimbursements (water), laundry, application fees, late fees, pet fees, parking, valet, trash, etc. These numbers can indicate issues with the property when you see late fees.

Expenses – Expenses from the normal operations of the property. Basically, this includes those things you have to do to keep the property going. This does not include debt or major capital improvements (new roof, for example).

NOI – VERY important calculation to understand. This represents the effective income, less operating expenses before debt payments. This figure is what determines the value of the property. Increase the NOI and you increase the price the next investor can pay for your property.

Cap Rate – This represents the rate of return the property would pay the investor if there was no debt on the property. It is calculated by subtracting expenses from effective gross income.

Effective Gross Income	$95,000
Expenses	$30,000
NOI	$65,000
Cap Rate	6.5%

If you pay $1,000,000 cash and the property was bought at a 6.5% cap rate, it would pay the investor $65,000 a year for their investment (6.5%) before the investor raises rents or improves operations by lowering expenses.

Leverage – This is referred to as the benefit the investor gains when they add debt to the return calculation, and it should improve investors' return. Leverage is only available if you can get great financing and great terms.

So, if I used debt in the example above, watch to see if the percentage return increases on the cash invested.

Effective Gross Income	$95,000		
Expenses	$30,000	Price	$1,000,000
NOI	$65,000	Down	$300,000
Debt Payment	<$39,000>	Debt	$700,000
Cash on Cash	$26,000	Cash%	8.66%
		(cash on cash / down payment)	

That is the value of leverage. The investor picked up two points by borrowing money from the bank. That may not seem like much, but you notice you were paid half the cash but only put down 30% of the money and have $700,000 left to invest in another deal or buy bigger deals.

When the interest rate you borrow at is lower than the cap rate, you will increase the return to the investor. The bigger the spread between the two, the bigger the return to the investor.

Cap Rate > Interest Rate = Increase In Return to Investor

Vacancy – The pro forma produced by the broker and also by the existing owner may show the amount of vacancy. This number is an abstract, almost meaningless number because if it is vacant it wasn't collected. However, by paying attention to it, you can learn the trends of the property.

Cash on Cash – The calculation based on the cash invested only. This is calculated by dividing the free cash by the cash put down to purchase. Free Cash / Down payment.

Cap Ex – The expenditure on those items not considered normal or recurring expenses to operate. A new roof or improvement of the clubhouse.

The Exit – How are you, as an owner, going to sell? This requires you to calculate what the next buyer can pay and still get a return on his investment. Lots of amateur investors miss this calculation because they only look at the calculations for operations and never figure out how to EXIT.

IO – Interest Only loans do exist in the market today, where you don't pay down the principal and only pay interest on the amount borrowed. If you put enough down at time of purchase, that is considered a principal paydown. You might even ask the bank if you increase your down payment at purchase how much IO they would give you. IO will provide you with more cash flow.

P&I – Principal and Interest refers to the main loan (principal) pay down and the interest paid to the lender for the loan. Each payment to the bank includes interest and some principal paydown that over the life of the loan will result in a zero balance when the loan completes its term.

Debt Coverage Ratio – This is a lender's term representing the fact that your income from operations is greater than the debt (P&I) you are paying the bank.

I will cover this more in an example. Let me show you what your first deal will look like.

First Deal Criteria - A to Z

These are some criteria you should use to evaluate your first deal. The more of these you can include in your first deal the better chance you have of finding a great deal.

A. 16 units or more (prefer 32). No matter how much you are tempted to buy smaller deals, the most important number in apartments is the number of units. This is your forced multiplier, also referred to as *"scaling."* Without scaling number of units, it is almost impossible to have a big score.

B. Love the property location when you first visit it. If you don't love it the second you walked on it, and have to make sense of how it will work, it will never work. Some properties just don't have whatever it takes. Avoiding bad deals is sometimes as important as finding the great ones. To develop this skill you must walk thousands of units to know the difference between something that makes money and you'll hate, and something that gushes money and you'll love. Also remember, love is required on the exit.

C. Be cash flow positive without improvements at 4% to 6% on cash invested. Cash flow is the holy grail of real estate investing and probably the least understood. Positive cash flow is what will determine your ability to hold the property during bad times, and by itself, determines the exit value.

D. Use debt on your first deal and no more than 75%. Don't pay cash for your apartments. This is not Dave Ramsey investing. The debt used to buy apartments is good debt and should be used over and over again. Never over-leverage and stay in the 65% to 75% debt-to-value range. Debt paid down by others is like a gift from the gods.

E. Have an active manager on property. You need someone on site thats knowledgeable and is paid well. Do not skimp on your manager. A manager that is underpaid will steal from you. Family members make bad managers. People that have been on properties for too long make bad managers. Even consider making your manager a sweat-equity owner in the property.

F. Have a 1.25% DCR (Debt Coverage Ratio). This DCR will probably be required by your bank, but never go below a 1.25% DCR. This means your NOI will exceed total debt by 25%. $100,000 worth of principal and interest would therefore require $125,000 worth of NOI.

G. Set aside $250 to $300 per unit per year for future renovation. This will also be required by the lender, but you should insist on at least this number annually set aside for unplanned property improvement.

H. Have an actual insurance quote. You should have an actual quote on your real estate before going under contract, not an estimate, but a firm quote. Also, check to be sure you're not in a flood zone.

I. Assume increase in property taxes at full rate. When calculating your taxes, you are best to estimate property taxes at the full price paid. Do not be tempted by real estate agents pro formas suggesting a percentage of the full price.

J. Use 40% or more as expense calculation. Any calculation used below this is naive and irresponsible. When making estimates, I will always use 40% to 50%, back of the napkin, as my worst case scenarios.

K. Assume no increase in effective gross income. The real estate agent and seller are going to try to convince you the property will produce higher rents in the future. While this is true, do not assume an increase in effective gross income. Better to be surprised in a positive way than disappointed because you were overly optimistic.

L. Have all obvious repair costs for next 36 months in reserve. Roofs, plumbing, siding, paint, parking, fences, walls; have it set aside. Never lose a piece of property because you can't take care of it. In 30 years, I have never lost a piece of property while my friends went broke. They thought I was being negative when I had 'set-asides' and I thought they were being stupid not having them.

M. Know break even occupancy (worst case scenario). When buying a deal, plan for worst case scenario and know what percent occupied gets you to a break even. Then look back over history and see if that property or that market has ever reached that occupancy level.

N. Know the financial statement by heart. You should not have to refer to the financial statement to understand the financial statement. I know the financial statements of my deals like I know the voice of my children; I don't need to see their face to know who I'm talking to.

O. Use a broker on the deal. If you don't use a broker you'll never get the best deal. Brokers are valuable connections to sellers and even more valuable to buyers when you exit. Never try to be your own broker to save a fee. I always use a broker to negotiate the buy or the sell.

P. Walk and create folders on at least 25 deals before you buy the first one. I look at hundreds of deals to buy one. Anything short of this is lazy and irresponsible. There is no book more valuable on real estate than walking deals and collecting folders. In the future, I will share with you what we put in our folders. The best education on your next deal is in all the deals you walked, collected data on and did not buy.

Q. Produce at least $24,000 a year regardless of Cash on Cash Percentage. Your first deal must produce at least $2,000 of net cash flow monthly for you to invest time or energy on it. The reason this is important is so you don't invest in deals too small and waste your time. If it doesn't make at least $24,000 a year, the target investment will be more of a bother than a solution.

R. Have minimal 25/50/75 rent increase potential. The property should be able to take a rent bump. If not, then you are buying something at full market rents and that would indicate you have no place to grow the property in the near future.

S. Have a solid exit plan for the property. The exit is vital to knowing how you will finally sell the property, or refinance it, and capture the upside of the property. Are you going to sell in 3 - 5 years? If so, then what is the expected price and how will that affect the returns?

T. Do an 8% exit calculation. Figure a price you can sell at that provides the new buyer with an 8% cash on cash return. What price can you sell at that will allow the new buyer to be able to make enough money to warrant his/her investment?

U. Have loan underwriting done by third party without the influence of your opinion of the deal. Have someone with underwriting experience look at the deal you are buying to determine how they see it.

V. Use worst case scenario on income. Do not be overly optimistic when it comes to future income. I never underwrite my deal with rent increases, even though I know they are coming. If your deal only makes sense if you get rent increases, it does not make sense and it will not make dollars.

W. Know the cost per door of expenses on the property in your market excluding taxes. Find the cost per door average in your market, and use that number to calculate, even if you know you can operate below that.

X. Underwrite your deal assuming all debt, including promises to partners, and all principal and interest when calculating for cash flow. Even if the lender or investors don't require principal paydown, underwrite your deal assuming they do.

Y. Assume 2 years of break even and no cash flow. This can happen and no one wants to confront these kinds of situations. You don't want to lose a great property because you weren't able to get through a couple of bad years. I have never lost a property because I always plan for worst case. Ask yourself, if this property broke even for a couple of years, would you still want to own it? If the answer is 'No Way,' don't buy it.

Z. By the time you have checked off each of the above, move on the deal, know that you have found a jewel, and buy the deal. The biggest mistake in real estate is not investing. The second biggest mistake is not moving fast enough when you find one.

You can always email me at: Deal@CardoneCapital.com and I will review your deal on my show, Real Estate Investing Made Simple.

Chapter 7

Cash On Cash (COC)

•

NO CALCULATION IS MORE IMPORTANT
THAN CASH FLOW – NONE!

Chapter 7

Cash On Cash (COC)

While most investors talk about price and cap rate when buying, there is no figure more important to me than cash on cash. How much unencumbered cash can be distributed to investors and myself after all operations and debts are handled. Positive cash flow, not just percentage, but the actual dollar amount of free cash flow after all operations, is what will allow you to weather economic pullbacks and avoid having to sell in down markets.

Positive cash flow is why I have never lost a property! When all the speculators and builders were losing everything during the worst housing crisis since the Great Depression, I held on to all my properties. Even the bank where I got my financing went down, but not me. Cash flow makes you bulletproof.

Imagine that! The bank that lent me money, busted out, and the apartment buildings never missed a payment to that bank. The bank made loans to a bunch of amateur speculators who over- leveraged, who didn't know how to calculate cash flow using worst case scenarios (or didn't bother to), and they all failed when the market got tough. I lost nothing, because I had cash flow.

When you have enough positive cash flow, you will be able to continue operations, while the competition across the street can no longer replace carpets or advertise.

Cash flow is the holy grail of businesses and what allows the business owner, in this case, the apartment owner, to continue operations. Cash flow provides confidence to the investor and is why Cardone Capital pays investors monthly, not quarterly.

My lawyer recommended I pay investors quarterly, suggesting it was more cost effective. I told the lawyer, *"I'm not paying for business advice, I'm paying you to put the agreement in place. I want to be paid every month and my partners deserve to be paid every month."* We collect rent every month, so why wouldn't I want to see cash from operations every month? I asked the lawyer, *"How would you like it if I only paid you four times a year?"*

No calculation is more important than cash flow – NONE! And your property should be able to distribute cash every month. Notice how big companies like AT&T and DIRECTV pay dividends to their investors every quarter if they can, but they bill customers every month. They do that because they can get away with it and that's why investing in real estate is better for you as long as you are able to generate positive cash flow monthly.

> No calculation is more important
> than cash flow – NONE!

This demand on cash flow forces the operator to not overpay, avoid over-leveraging and neglecting or mismanaging operations. Violate the demand on cash flow in your underwriting and you will end up in trouble.

Also, understand, the value of the apartment doesn't go up and down without reason. Unlike a home, the value of apartments and office buildings are determined by the cash flow they produce. The third reason cash flow is important is the apartments' cash flow provides a protection against the devaluation of cash.

But, the biggest reason I insist that my partners at Cardone Capital are paid monthly is that it builds confidence. My friend Howard, an investor in multiple deals with me, once said, *"The cash flow is not really important to me."* After about 4 months of distributions, he called me and said, *"I have to tell you, getting that little check, $10,000 every month, really makes me feel good."*

The banks and insurance companies validate why apartments are dependable investments. Banks and insurance companies have lent me hundreds of millions of dollars to buy apartments, but won't lend me money to buy their own company stock or to buy their own products. Read that again and let it sink in: Banks will lend me money to buy apartments but will not lend me money to buy their own stock. Why? Because the apartments produce cash flow and the stock of the bank does not.

In fact, it is easier to get a loan on an apartment deal than a single-family home. Banks typically love apartments, and they are the favored asset class to lend on today because they have proven the ability to produce positive cash flow through all types of economic conditions. A real asset that produces cash flow will appreciate in value over time. Apartments are land deals with a cash flow positive business sitting above them.

BANKS WILL LEND ME MONEY TO BUY APARTMENTS BUT WILL NOT LEND ME MONEY TO BUY THEIR OWN STOCK.

The cash flow component is so important to the lender, they base the amount of the loan on the properties ability to produce cash. The lender will only loan you an amount equivalent to some portion of the NOI. This is called DCR or Debt Coverage Ratio.

I believe the DCR calculation is more important than the appraisal, the price paid, cap rate, or the percentage of your down payment. The Debt Coverage Ratio, normally 1.25%, suggests the amount of the principal and interest covered by the Net Operating Income (income less expenses) equals no less than 125%. If the properties debt is $100,000 a year, the NOI would need to be $125,000, if the bank required a 1.25% DCR. The lower the DCR, the more the lender likes the property and the borrower.

THE CASH FLOW COMPONENT IS SO IMPORTANT TO THE LENDER THEY BASE THE AMOUNT OF THE LOAN ON THE PROPERTIES ABILITY TO PRODUCE CASH.

So, once you know your NOI and you understand the DCR underwriting of your lender, you can pretty much estimate how much principal and interest the lender will allow you to have. Then, you can back into how much they lend you.

NOI		$1,000,000
DCR	(divide)	1.25%
Annual P&I		$800,000
Interest		4.5%
Principal Amount Allowed		$13,677,000

(Use mortgage calculators loan amount)

If you need help figuring out a deal you are looking at, email me at: Deal@CardoneCapital.com and I'll walk you through it. Who knows, if it fits the other criteria, I might buy it with you.

Chapter 8

Where to Find Deals

•

THE FASTEST WAY TO GET DEALS IS TO CLOSE
ON THE DEALS YOU MAKE OFFERS ON.

Chapter 8

Where to Find Deals

The place to start is where you know the market, code for: where you live. Don't try to go into new markets in the beginning, shop where you live and stay close to where you live until you start to learn the market. The first market I ever shopped was within a 10 mile radius of where I lived. For 3 years, every weekend, when I wasn't working my main job, I shopped deals, exhausting every broker in the market, and I never bought a deal.

But, I got a great education and I learned what a good deal looked and felt like. I realized after leaving Houston to move to California, how much money I would have made had I invested. I saw what I thought were a lot of good deals, but I wasn't ready yet. I didn't have the confidence yet, because I hadn't yet done enough homework to KNOW enough to know the difference between a bad deal, a good deal, and a screaming deal. What you learn from walking properties is 10 times more valuable than what you will learn reading a book.

When I moved to San Diego, I realized I had learned a lot and walked away from some very good deals, but rather than regretting what I didn't buy, I resumed shopping properties in the new market I had moved to. The difference was, this time, I had the confidence of KNOWING what I was doing, what I was looking for, what a good deal looked and felt like, and what a bad deal looked and felt like. The bad ones are easy to know. You immediately know it doesn't work and you don't spend time trying to make sense of it. If it doesn't feel good, I don't buy it.

I was only in San Diego a year when I bought my first deal. It was 48 units in Vista, California. I still remember driving up to it the first time. It was two stories, had great presence from the road, looked like it was quality build, nice space between the parking lot, the street and the units, and I knew immediately I would buy it.

I closed the deal in 45 days and 30 days later, I bought another 38 units in Point Loma. 90 days after that I bought my third true rental deal. A 92 unit, C Class, value-add beauty.

Within 3 years, I had collected 500 units. Over the last 25 years, I have since bought and sold over $1 billion worth of real estate, in 8 different markets, through all types of economic climates.

What I know today after doing this for years is:

1) Apartments are the best investment for protecting your capital, providing dependable cash flow, and appreciation over long periods of time.

2) It's vital to know the market you are investing in today and looking forward over the next 5 to 10 years.

3) Knowing the market starts with knowing where the deals are and who has them.

4) The brokers who have the deals you want are CBRE, ARA, Cushman Wakefield, Marcus & Millichap, Berkshire, HFF and a few private broker shops in each market. Of course, there are also the private sellers. By having the right technology, you can get access to the broker property intel and the data is priceless.

How you contact those brokers and what you say to them is too much for this introduction, as that is an art in and of itself.

I learned very quickly, the fastest way to get deals is to close on the deals you make offers on. Be a closer, stay true to your word, and never violate the trust of the brokers' market. Once the market knows you are a real buyer (a closer) the game of creating wealth through real estate investing becomes possible. The broker network is very small, and in most markets, only a few guys control all of the apartment inventory, at least the good stuff. If they don't believe in your ability to close, you will never get the good deals.

THE FASTEST WAY TO GET DEALS IS TO CLOSE
ON THE DEALS YOU MAKE OFFERS ON.

The brokers are very private, highly competitive, almost paranoid, and, for the most part, underpaid. If they don't know you, they won't even return your phone call. Once you get them on the phone you better be able to validate your story as a buyer.

Also, always deal with the listing broker. Whoever controls the listing, controls the deal. Find out who is controlling the inventory in your market. Just because a broker is the big guy in one market, doesn't mean they represent well in another.

The next thing is, you have to know the market. When I say *"Know the market,"* this is what I mean: economics, job providers, rents, concessions, expenses, the growing parts of the market, dying parts of markets, the politics of the city, the home prices in the area, the overall economic conditions, occupancy, cost

How To Create Wealth Investing In Real Estate • *CardoneCapital.com*   151

of insurance, flood zones, salaries, crime rates, walk scores, reviews, concessions, credit worthiness of the market, demographics of your tenants, competition, other sales, history of property going back 5 years or longer; everything and more.

You should know what the last buyer paid for the deal you are considering, and know how the property operated during the bad times. You must know the existing management company's work ethic, and service, to unveil opportunities.

You should walk the property during the day, at night, and on the weekends. You should also mystery shop the property in person and over the phone.

When you are investing, there is a lot to research: KNOW, don't guess. Listen to everyone, ask a lot of questions, but make sure you know what the reality is, not someone's opinion. As Ronald Reagan made the Russian proverb famous, *"Trust but verify."*

Chapter 9

Why I Created
Cardone Capital

•

THE ENTIRE SYSTEM IS STACKED
AGAINST THE LITTLE GUY.

Chapter 9

Why I Created Cardone Capital

I originally created Cardone Capital to give others access to the deals I am doing. For 30 years, I have been investing in real estate without other investors. My twin brother was the first to ask if he could invest alongside me, then my sister did. Soon, word got around about the great returns I was getting and some close friends, and some of my best customers, also wanted in on the deals too. For the most part, all of these people were either very high net worth individuals or close friends and family.

Last year, I was persuaded by my real estate team to create a fund to allow those outside my close relationships to invest with me. We thought this was good for them, giving them access to deals they couldn't get without me, and it would allow us to scale our real estate business.

We launched Cardone Capital and created a vehicle whereby qualified investors (the wealthy) could invest alongside me. Our first three offerings were over-subscribed, meaning more people wanted to invest than we had room for. We raised over $58 million and bought a almost $200 million of apartments that produce passive income for me and our investors.

While engaging with legal to create the funds, I was repeatedly asked, *"How do we get the little guy involved in my deals?"* I was told over and over by legal, *"Don't open this up to everyone, you are just inviting trouble."* Every time I heard this I knew it was wrong. My whole life I have been the little guy and I have always pulled for the little guy. As I dug into why this was, I became aware of the complexities of the system and how the entire system is stacked against the little guy.

The non-accredited investor is encouraged to buy a single-family home or maybe a duplex or fourplex, but the moment he or she tries to get bigger, then the system (banks and legal) tighten up against them. This prevents the very individuals who need this wealth-creating vehicle the most, from investing at all. The single mother raising two kids needs a place to put her money where it won't be lost, provides passive income, the possibility of appreciation in the future, and the tax advantages used by the wealthy. I wondered, *"Why are they making it so hard for the non-accredited investor to invest?"*

THE ENTIRE SYSTEM IS STACKED AGAINST THE LITTLE GUY.

I remembered earlier in my career how hard it was when I started trying to buy bigger deals. The great deals were either never shown to me or never awarded to me. It was very difficult to get the debt. It was also difficult to convince the lender I could manage the bigger deals. Funny thing is, the bigger deals are easier to manage than the little deals, which are almost impossible to manage. I watched the big players get awarded the trophy properties and I would basically buy the stuff they didn't want.

You can still make money like that, but it means you must be in the market every day working in real estate. The average person trying to pay the bills and take care of their family can't be out there every day competing to buy deals in the marketplace. So, the little guy is left to buy a duplex or convince themselves that owning a home is owning real estate (NOT). Then you will see hoards of people flipping (wholesaling) single-family homes, which is not investing but rather speculating. One of my in-laws bought a small deal in Oakland and found she didn't have the time or the skill to manage the tenants and ended up losing the property.

Vanguard, Blackstone, Goldman (Wall Street) and banks are buying the best real estate in America and holding them for long periods of time. The rest of America is encouraged to buy a home or a duplex and get a loan from the banks, or invest in a REIT (a piece of paper created by Vanguard, Blackstone or Goldman).

At best, the little guy might get an offering from a local real estate syndicator offering a 30 unit apartment deal that needs to be rehabbed or one of the popular crowdsourcing sites that offer an *"opportunity"* to invest in a marina or a single-family home in Covina, California.

When I realized this, I committed to doing something about it. I hired an attorney to create a fund where my high net worth friends and non-accredited friends, followers, and employees, could all invest with me in the real estate deals I'm doing. The lawyer warned me, *"Grant, do not open this to the little guy,"* and then she went on to give me two reasons why:

1) It is very expensive and takes a long time.
2) Non-accredited investors are only trouble.

It wasn't expensive or difficult to allow my family and close friends to invest with me and it hasn't been trouble. I do all the work, they put in their money with mine, sign an agreement saying they understand they are passive investors, and I send them money every month. I asked the lawyer, *"Who is making it so hard for people who want to invest with me?"*

The lawyer went on to explain it was the government's job to protect the little investor. I knew this was not the reason because the government can't protect the little guy even if they wanted to. I also knew that just because someone makes a lot of money doesn't make them financially smarter.

Financial intelligence has nothing to do with earning power, think Mike Tyson, Nick Cage, Mark Twain, or bankrupt businessmen Abe Lincoln, H.J. Heinz, Henry Ford, Larry King, and Dave Ramsey. What about the number of financial institutions who failed with their floors of Harvard graduates like WorldCom, Tyco, Lehman, IndyMac, and Washington Mutual?

So I kept asking, *"Who doesn't want the little guy to invest with me when I know these deals are good for them?"* I called a friend of mine who used to work on Wall Street and asked him, *"Why does Wall Street make it so hard for the little guy to invest with me?"* He said, *"Grant, 97% of the US population is non-accredited. The big boys want that investor for themselves."*

He was right. It cost me almost 30X more to have legal create a fund for non-accredited investors. When I say the deck is stacked against the little guy, I am not being dramatic. To get approval for me to raise money from the *"little guy"* it can cost more than $500,000 and take six months. To create a fund for the wealthy, less than 3% of the population, it costs $15,000 and takes two weeks.

Wall Street doesn't want to compete with Grant Cardone, Wall Street wants you, or they want to stay as the middleman between you and a company like mine. You see, these guys will buy all my real estate in the future, keep me on as the manager/operator and immediately turn the whole company into a REIT (Real Estate Investment Trust) that is paper stock, not real estate.

We've all heard of derivatives, IPOs, REITs, and ETFs and were made to believe they are so good for us when in truth they all are just a bunch of casino games. The laws are set up to protect Wall Street, not the little guy, and it's an attempt to control the money of 97% of all investors.

Wall Street wants the best deals for themselves, so they make it cost prohibitive for others to create investment opportunities for the little guy. The rich get richer because the wealthy have access to the best deals and the little guy stays little because he never gets access to the bigger deals. Think I am exaggerating? To be a customer of Goldman Sachs you need a minimum of $10 million in cash but their average client has $50 million.

> THE LITTLE GUY STAYS LITTLE BECAUSE HE
> NEVER GETS ACCESS TO THE BIGGER DEALS.

I am going to change the game of how the little guy invests in real estate. I am investing my time and money to create funds for ALL people to partner with me on trophy real estate. Whether you are accredited or non-accredited we are cutting out Wall Street— the middleman—and giving my friends, family, and followers access to deals that are typically reserved for the wealthiest organizations on the planet. By the way, every accredited investor was at one time a non-accredited investor. Most of my life I could not even qualify to invest in my own funds.

I thought about calling it the *"Little Guy Fund"* but instead we decided to name it Cardone Equity Fund V, because it's our fifth offering. To be involved all you have to do is register at CardoneCapital.com. We are proposing a $10,000 minimum to the SEC and are waiting for their approval so it's not yet determined what the limits will be. By the time you read this, we should be up and running and all that will be determined. We have already had tens of thousands of people hear about this and show interest.

Just so you understand, my entire life I have been helping people. My purpose and mission is to help people. I have also always been a disrupter to the status quo. Up until a few years ago, what I am doing here with real estate wasn't even possible, but now it is. I don't need to raise money to continue to amass my own wealth in real estate, but want to extend the opportunity to help you, the accredited and non-accredited alike, to partner with you to take on Wall Street and disrupt the financial institutions and level the playing field.

I have the connections to find and buy deals in every market. I am also preferred and a highly trusted borrower with the biggest lenders in the world, and I'm able to access the best credit terms available. My borrowing limits at this time, we think, are somewhere in the three billion range, but we have a good idea that will be raised as soon as we hit it. I find the deals, finance them, sign on them, and manage them, while you invest with me!

I recently assumed the loan on 800 units in Nashville, where the bank allowed me to take over the existing portfolio's debt of $58 million without having to get a new loan. Ryan Tseko, my pilot, sold his 18 single-family units in Arizona and invested with me, and rather than owning 100% of 18 units he owned a small percentage of 823 units. I bought the portfolio for $58 million and was just offered $90 million, turning Ryan's $400,000 into $1.2 million.

My sister Diane Cardone, a non-accredited investor at that time, invested most of her retirement and 401k savings with me in a thousand unit portfolio. This has been a game changer for her by providing her with passive income in excess of any job she ever held while she waited patiently to find out her investment is worth 4X more.

Just this year, we have bought almost 1,500 units in four locations. One was an off-market deal (not listed for sale) in Houston, Texas, from one of the largest apartment owners in the world. I knew the person to contact, in the dispositions department, and 90 days later I closed a world class location totaling 507 units. Two weeks later I got a call about a property in Orlando across from the Ritz-Carlton Hotel. The broker gave me the inside track on the deal because he knows I can close, and this resulted in 240 units totaling $51 million.

We have the management team in place with almost 150 employees across the country, managing the properties and delivering the Cardone Customer Experience to potential tenants. The profile of our average person interested is someone who loves real estate, works full time, has a family, likes the idea of monthly distributions and is willing and able to wait for appreciation but simply doesn't have the time required to find and manage deals.

That being said, Cardone Capital even has other professional real estate groups investing with us in our funds. For example, Bobby C, who personally owns one thousand units on his own, recently invested $1.5 million into 700 units I bought.

Jarrod Glandt, VP of Sales at Cardone Enterprises, with a new marriage and a baby boy, along with a full-time job, doesn't have time to find and manage real estate on his own. He started investing with me four years ago. Today, he earns more passive income from his investments with me than he does from his job and is already a millionaire at the age of 35.

I can't promise our past performance will equal the future, but I can tell you this: I believe in the real estate we are investing in and want to help you be part of it.

Most of those who have registered with CardoneCapital. com or call my weekly Real Estate show say, *"I don't have time to find deals, call brokers, negotiate purchase and sale agreements, hire lawyers, and manage tenants."* So, if that is you and you are interested, check out what we are doing at CardoneCapital.com where we invest in cash flow producing properties in markets with job growth that favor migration of both the baby boomer population and the millennials. We only invest in apartments we are willing to hold for a period of 10 years or longer with the goal to 2X - 3X our investment.

Our deal size is $30 million to $200 million involving 200 to 1,000 units. We use debt on every deal whereby I arrange all debt based on my connections and reputation. I negotiate all the terms of purchase, sale, and debt, and am fully responsible, leaving investors with no exposure to the debt obligation. We typically use 50% to 75% debt leverage with a hold time that is discretionary, meaning we are not forced to sell in a bad market.

So, if you love real estate be sure to register at CardoneCapital.com. We will take investors on a first to register basis.

In Closing

In Closing

Whether you invest with me at Cardone Capital, or on your own, make a decision to start investing your money in real estate. This move to cash flow producing real estate will continue to be a great investment over time, as nothing can stop it. There is no technology that can possibly disrupt the fact that people need affordable places to live.

Get your money out of the banks and the stock market. Your money is dying at the bank, depreciating at a faster rate than what the banks pay you, by almost 6 times. The stock market offers more drama than profits. Invest in hard assets that produce positive cash flow while you wait for the property to appreciate. Money in your house is not an investment; at best, it is equity sitting in your house, dead.

The money you have in paper stocks, ETFs and mutual funds is making Wall Street rich and doing next to nothing for you and the day of reckoning is coming. At any time, your investment can get cut in half or go to zero. Your IRA, SEP, and Keogh money is being almost completely ignored, where the investor gets a report once a quarter and no monthly cash flow to live on.

The income property business is a simple business where you find someone to live or work at the real estate you own. It is a business that has a proven track record to protect capital, produce cash flow, appreciate over time, and is a great hedge against inflation.

Of all my businesses, none of them have provided me with more financial security than real estate. While it is a simple business, it is not an easy business, nor is it a get rich quick vehicle. Like any investment, real estate has risks, but when done correctly and you know where you are investing, you have a great chance of succeeding.

Do the math: What other investment allows you to invest $100,000 and get $300,000 in assets? What investment pays you every month while you wait for the income on the property to pay the debt down to zero? What investment can you make today where the income from the investment is taxed at the lowest rates? What investment exists that provides for you to write off 100% of the interest payments and accelerate the depreciation of the physical assets of the property?

Once you understand what I know about real estate, you will have a responsibility to either start buying your own deals or investing with someone who knows what they are doing.

Understanding the Real Estate Formula

CASH FLOW X UNITS + TIME = APPRECIATION

At Cardone Capital this is how we view our investments and calculate the investments of our partners:

Every $1 million buys a $3 million deal.

6% Cash Flow - ($60,000 x 10 years) =	$600,000
3.5% Appreciation per year x 10 years =	$1,000,000
1.5% Debt Pay Down per year (15%) =	$300,000
Original Investment Return at sale =	$1,000,000
Total	$2,900,000

Pay close attention to the magic of multiplication and leverage. Remember, we only invested $1 million and the property only has to increase by $1 million to give us a 100% return.

Because of leverage, notice the property didn't have to double in value for us to double our investment and that gain is before the consideration of cash on cash.

The 6% cash on cash returned us 60% of our capital and that assumes no rent increases. Add to that, the simple 3.5% appreciation over 10 years, and that means the property and our $1 million investment is worth $1.6 million, or 60% return.

Don't think these returns are unusual, in fact, what I showed you above is very conservative. Later, I will include some of the deals we are currently invested in and show you how they are doing at this time. In our fund, Cardone Capital, we avoid the mistakes the little investors make. We buy large deals in great locations, have the properties professionally managed, get the best debt in the world, and never over-leverage. Then, we pay attention to the property and allow time to do its magic while the investors are paid monthly.

We do the research, shop the deals, negotiate the purchase, the sale and the financing, buy the deal with my money and my credit, and then, investors come along to partner with me on the gains. We don't win until you do, and the more you win, the more we win. I want my partners praying at night, *"Make sure GC makes a lot of money."* When I make money, you make money and when you make money, I make money and scale my business. We are literally changing the way people invest in real estate. No small deals, no Section 8, no bad locations, no tenant issues, no phone calls, and all the benefits of real estate.

While all investments have risks, leaving your money in the banks and at Wall Street, also has risks. The people who lost the most money during the worst real estate crash in our history were homeowners and small investors.

Looking forward, it would be a good guess that properties which provide positive cash flow, in good locations, will be worth more 10 years from now, and even more still, 20 years from now, than they are today. Look into the future, to 2028 or 2038, and you will only wish you had invested more in properties in good locations.

The power of leverage is hard to understand until you start benefiting from it, but consider my first deal was $350,000 that today provides my family with millions of dollars each month in income and over 1 billion dollars in property.

In 10 years, the rents in Miami, Houston, Orlando, Savannah, will probably be a great deal higher than they are today; not 30% higher but probably closer to 100% higher. A $1,500 two bedroom in Houston or Orlando today, could easily be closer to $3,000 in 10 years. The more the rents rise, the more valuable the property becomes, and the more cash flow to the investors.

It would be an understatement to say I am bullish on apartments, the reality is, I have 95% of my wealth invested in the type of real estate I have been describing here. For 30 years, even through the worst economies, cash flow producing real estate, in good locations, has never let me down.

Real estate is what has provided me with the lifestyle and freedom I am experiencing today and can do the same for you and your family. Even when my other businesses were cut in half during the economic collapse, the real estate kept cash flowing.

More importantly, when I go to sleep at night, I am not concerned about losing my investment. This very specific type of real estate provides me with complete certainty and assurance I will not lose my initial capital and that my family, church, charities, and the things I love, will be funded, even when I am unable to work or no longer around.

Consider the first deal I did in multi-family: I invested $350,000 to buy a $1.95 million, 48 unit complex. I can't lose my money as it is invested in the property. Because of leverage, I was able to buy a $1.95 million asset that produced $40,000 of positive cash flow a year while I waited for appreciation. 39 months later, I sold the property for $5.2 million resulting in a total profit before taxes of $3.7 million. That is a 10X return.

$350,000 down	$1,950,000	(48 unit complex)
Sold	$5,200,000	(39 months)
Payoff Debt	$1,600,000	
Remaining	$3,600,000	
Cash Flow (39 months)	$130,000	

$350,000 turned into $3,730,000

10X return in 39 months.

I made more money on this one deal than I had made at all the jobs I had ever held and my first two businesses combined. Now the issue was: how many more times could I do this?

Remember, to create wealth you can't just score once, you must be able to repeat it. This is called scaling. Scaling (repeating) scores is critical to creating wealth. Can you do it over and over again? This is why wholesaling doesn't work and why the stock market is an awful gamble. Even when you win, you know it is difficult to repeat. To assure you this can be repeated, I included all the deals I have done in my career at the end of the book.

Now, if you can't start with $350,000 like I did, then start with what you have and raise money, but do not do small deals; they don't work.

IT IS BETTER TO OWN 1% OF A SUCCESSFUL DEAL THAN 100% OF A DEAL THAT NEVER MAKES MONEY AND TAKES UP ALL OF YOUR TIME.

Either raise money so you can do the bigger deals, or start investing now with someone doing bigger deals, and get your money multiplying. It is better to own 1% of a successful deal than 100% of a deal that never makes money and takes up all of your time.

How to Turn $10,000 into $1,000,000

My whole life I have been fascinated with money. I dreamed, as a kid, what it would be like to be wealthy, have the freedom to travel the world, and take care of my family, but mostly, to not have to worry about money.

I have spent 30 years trying to demystify the calculations and understand how to control the outcome. I discovered this formula called *the future value of money*, whereby an individual can calculate the future value of an investment depending on what the money earns over time. What I quickly discovered was, to create wealth you need a vehicle that multiplies money. The banks don't multiply money; the money just sits there and depreciates, earning less than inflation. The stock market puts your money at risk and violates the first rule of investing, *"Never lose money."*

To create wealth, you cannot simply hope or pray, you need a plan and you need the right vehicle. Money will not multiply just because you have a job or own a business. You must find vehicles that provide the multiplying effect.

The Future Value of Money Calculation

The future value of money is defined as *"The value of an asset or cash in the future that is equivalent to a sum today."* Assume you invest $10,000 and want to know the future value of the money. The future value will be determined by how much the money earns each year. Does your investment earn 1%, 6%, 10% or more?

To put this into perspective, today the banks pay ¼ of 1% on monies sitting in checking accounts and money markets. Yes, you read that correctly: One fourth of one percent and the national average at banks is .0012%. Wall Street claims (not to be trusted) the average return on stocks in the market, over the last 20 years, is 6%. At Cardone Capital, we look for properties we believe will return 15% internal rate of return including cash flow and appreciation (before taxes) and have exceeded those numbers on every deal we have ever done. Whether I can continue to do that in the future is unknown, but when you learn how to use the future value of money calculator, you will understand I don't need to. The goal is to multiply money, not hit a certain percentage.

So, watch me show you how to multiply $10,000 using the future value of money calculation. We will start with a $10,000 investment and never add to that investment to see what $10,000 will be worth in the future.

Investment	%	Term	Future Value	
a) $10,000	1%	10	$11,046	(Bank pays ¼ of 1%)
b) $10,000	6%	10	$17,908	1.7X
c) $10,000	10%	10	$25,937	2.5X
d) $10,000	15%	10	$40,455	(projected Cardone Capital)
e) $10,000	20%	10	$61,917	6.1X
f) $10,000	25%	10	$93,132	9.1X

Keep in mind, the first entry is 4X what banks actually pay on checking accounts and money markets. When you leave $10,000 at the bank you would earn $2.50 in 12 months. $10,000 would become $10,002.50.

Even at the minimal 6% cash flow returns we expect

from our deals, when compared to a 1% return, your money grew 1.7X. Not great, but 60% more than leaving your money at the bank or in cash accounts at Merrill Lynch or Fidelity.

Now, get into the realm of returns we look to achieve at Cardone Capital; you will notice when using the future value of money it all gets really interesting. Our expectation on investments we are making today are in the 15% to 25% range, including cash flow and the sale of the property. Look at entry (d) and you will see your money has grown 4X, or 400%, from $10,000 to $40,000 compared to earning $1,000 at the 1%.

This would assume cash distributions, plus appreciation upon selling the property, before depreciation and taxes. When you look at the end of this chapter, you will see deals I have been doing for years that exceed 15%.
Now, consider what happens when you start with the same $10,000, as in the earlier examples, but then add $10,000 once a year for each of the 10 years:

Investment	Add/Yearly	%	Term	Future Value
$10,000	$10,000	15%	10	$243,492

Now, I said I would show you how to turn $10,000 into $1,000,000, so here you go. Earn 15% on your investment and you will see your investment turn into over $1,000,000. If you invested $10,000 a year for 20 years for a total of $200,000 invested, you would walk away with $1.188 million before taxes:

Investment	Add/Yearly	%	Term	Future Value
$10,000	$10,000	15%	20	$1,188,101
$10,000	$10,000	20%	20	$2,250,256

If you find an asset that produces 20% return, between cash flow and appreciation, your $200,000 investment is worth $2,250,256. Again, this is before taxes, but now you're really multiplying money.

If you are highly skeptical, you will have to go over the numbers a few times, but numbers don't lie. The question you need to ask yourself is, *"Where can I get 15% to 20% returns year after year without the risk of losing my capital investment?"* This isn't witchcraft, hype, or fluff, these are real numbers produced from real assets. That is the beauty of real estate. You can see it, touch it, people live in it, and use it. No technology today can replace it and it has proven itself as a dependable investment for thousands of years.

That, is why I pick multi-family real estate. When rents go up, the cash flow increases. Ask yourself, *"Will rents be higher 10 years from now?"* I don't need a crystal ball. They will be higher. And when cash flow increases, the next buyer will pay a premium for our property when we decide to sell, at which point we multiply our money. Add to that, when inflation rears its head, it makes real assets worth more money.

It takes real money down to buy the great assets, that is why the big boys get all the great real estate, and the little guys end up with the left overs. I am changing this at Cardone Capital, allowing you to invest alongside me on the big deals you will never see on your own.

Now, if you are out there and run into a deal too big for you that fits the criteria I laid out earlier in the book, reach out to me; maybe I will buy it with you.

Lastly, to create wealth you must 1) make a commitment 2) have a plan 3) have a vehicle to invest in and 4) avoid losses. I use real estate to do this for me and if you elect to do the same, I pray real estate investing is as good for you as it has been for me, my family, and our investors at Cardone Capital.

Grant Cardone
CEO, Cardone Capital

Do me a favor...

If you haven't written a review yet I would really appreciate if you did so for me right now. There is nothing an author likes more than a REVIEW. Go to GrantCardone.com/realestatebook and write your review. We love five stars and great comments.

Investors who don't want to do your own deals: By the time you read this book I will be approved to have both accredited and non-accredited investors partner with me on big deals like the ones I describe here. Go to CardoneCapital.com or call 310-777-0255.

I won't let you down because I refuse to let me down.

Thanks for being interested in learning more, and remember if you ever land a deal too big to take down by yourself send it to me or call-in to our weekly real estate show at the Cardone Zone, also available on iTunes.

And don't forget to follow me on YOUR favorite social media site, just punch in @grantcardone.

Great investing,
GC

Real Estate Calculator Terms & Definitions

Real Estate – Property consisting of land or buildings.

Purchase Price – The price of the property plus all closing cost, legal fees, document fees, etc, finances cost and rehab.

Down Payment – The amount used to fund the acquisition less the debt.

Debt Coverage Ratio -The debt divided by the NOI. This number is typically 1.10 to 1.25 depending on the asset class and borrower.

Loan Term – The period you need to pay the loan. Typically apartment deals are amortized over thirty years with a payoff due at the 10 year mark.

Interest Rate – The proportion of a loan that is charged as interest to the borrower, usually expressed as an annual percentage of the loan outstanding.

P&I – Principal and Interest includes the interest on the loan amount plus paying down the principal monthly.

Principal – Denoting an original sum invested as the down payment.

Interest – Money paid regularly at a particular rate for the use of money borrowed.

Closing Costs – Fees paid at the closing of a real estate transaction.

Vacancy Rate – A value calculated as the percentage of all available units in a rental property that are vacant or unoccupied at a particular time.

Gross Scheduled Income – The maximum possible annual income generated by rent collections.

Occupancy Rate – The number of the units occupied at the property.

Economic Occupancy – the percentage of units that the property is actually collecting rent on. This number is much more valuable to me than occupancy rate.

Other Income – All the other income generated from the property which could include parking, laundry, late payments, storage, etc.

Property Management Expense – The total expenses for maintaining the property.

Capitalization Rate – The ratio between the Net Operating Income (NOI) produced by an asset and its capital cost (the original price paid to buy the asset); or, its current market value.

Cash on Cash – The return on investment of the monies invested. It is equal to the Before Tax Cash Flow (BTCF) divided by the sum of all out-of- pocket acquisition costs (down payment, closing costs, etc.).

Gross Rent Multiplier – Purchase Price divided by the Gross Scheduled Income (GSI). The lower this number the better.

Net Income Multiplier – Purchase Price divided by the Net Operating Income (NOI). The lower the number the better.

Debt Coverage Ratio – The Net Operating Income (NOI) divided by the Annual Debt Service. The higher the number the better.

Expense Ratio – Total Operating Expense divided by Gross Operating Income (GOI), expressed as a percentage. A percentage below 35 is considered good.

Assets Under
Cardone Management

Harbour Breeze - 100% Funded

Location	Stuart, FL
Units	104
Purchase Price	$5,000,000
Projected IRR	27%

Harbour Pines - 100% Funded

Location	St. Lucie, FL
Units	152
Purchase Price	$8,500,000
Projected IRR	29%

Harbour Palms - 100% Funded

Location	St. Lucie, FL
Units	244
Purchase Price	$12,500,000
Projected IRR	31%

Harbour Cay South - 100% Funded

Location	Stuart, FL
Units	112
Purchase Price	$7,200,000
Projected IRR	34%

Harbour Cay - 100% Funded

Location	Stuart, FL
Units	272
Purchase Price	$20,800,000
Projected IRR	33%

Harbour Bay - 100% Funded

Location	Palm Bay, FL
Units	236
Purchase Price	$10,500,000
Projected IRR	26%

Jackson Grove - 100% Funded

Location	Nashville, TN
Units	238
Purchase Price	$19,000,000
Projected IRR	33%

Lincoya Bay - 100% Funded

Location	Nashville, TN
Units	186
Purchase Price	$14,800,000
Projected IRR	33%

Sheffield Heights - 100% Funded

Location	Nashville, TN
Units	202
Purchase Price	$16,500,000
Projected IRR	35%

Hickory Creek - 100% Funded

Location	Nashville, TN
Units	200
Purchase Price	$13,800,000
Projected IRR	26%

Audobon Park - 100% Funded

Location	Daphne, AL
Units	344
Purchase Price	$34,000,000
Projected IRR	24%

The Trellis - 100% Funded

Location	Savannah, GA
Units	264
Purchase Price	$29,000,000
Projected IRR	19%

Integra Shores - 100% Funded

Location	Daytona, FL
Units	288
Purchase Price	$32,200,000
Projected IRR	25%

Realm - 100% Funded

Location	Boca Raton, FL
Units	102
Purchase Price	$12,800,000
Projected IRR	15%

Wellington Club - 100% Funded

Location	Lake Worth, FL
Units	204
Purchase Price	$31,950,000
Projected IRR	18%

Heron Pointe - 100% Funded

Location	Boynton Beach, FL
Units	192
Purchase Price	$30,400,000
Projected IRR	14%

Reserve at Port St. Lucie - 100% Funded

Location	St. Lucie, FL
Units	188
Purchase Price	$19,500,000
Projected IRR	15%

Reserve at Ormond Beach - 100% Funded

Location	Ormond Beach, FL
Units	272
Purchase Price	$36,500,000
Projected IRR	15%

Cardone Equity Fund III - 100% Funded

Location	Orlando, FL & Houston, TX
Units	747
Purchase Price	$100,000,000+
Projected IRR	12-15%

About
Grant Cardone

About Grant Cardone

Grant Cardone is a New York Times bestselling author, international social media influencer, the number one sales trainer in the world, and an internationally renowned speaker on leadership, real estate, investing, entrepreneurship, social media, and finance. He is a regular guest on Fox News, Fox Business, CNBC, and MSNBC. He is also a contributing writer for Forbes, Success Magazine, Business Insider, Entrepreneur.com and the Huffington Post.

Mr. Cardone founded and leads Cardone Capital which currently has 5,000 units under ownership and over one billion dollars in real estate holdings.

Cardone Capital is changing the way people invest in multi-family real estate. Cardone has spent over 25 years focusing on investing in income-producing, affordable housing in the secondary and tertiary markets. Cardone Capital has successfully offered accredited funds in the past with positive returns and margins on all. Now offering non-accredited fund opportunities to everyday investors, Cardone Capital continues to further its legacy as a disrupter having cutting-edge approaches to investments and creating wealth.

Take the next step, learn more, and invest with Grant Cardone himself through Cardone Capital.

Interested accredited investors register at: CardoneCapital.com/invest

Interested non-accredited investors register at: CardoneCapital.com/fund